ESSENTIAL SOCIAL SKILLS FOR TEENS

THE ULTIMATE GUIDE TO NAVIGATE SOCIAL MEDIA, MANAGE PEER-PRESSURE, IMPROVE SELF-CONFIDENCE, OVERCOME SOCIAL ANXIETY, AND CREATE LASTING RELATIONSHIPS

JORDAN WIZE

Copyright © 2024 Jordan Wize. All rights reserved.

The content within this book may not be reproduced, duplicated, or transmitted without direct written permission from the author or the publisher.

Under no circumstances will any blame or legal responsibility be held against the publisher or author for any damages, reparation, or monetary loss due to the information contained within this book, either directly or indirectly.

Legal Notice:

This book is copyright-protected. It is only for personal use. You cannot amend, distribute, sell, use, quote, or paraphrase any part of this book's content without the author's or publisher's consent.

Disclaimer Notice:

Please note the information contained within this document is for educational and entertainment purposes only. All effort has been expended to present accurate, up-to-date, reliable, and complete information. No warranties of any kind are declared or implied. Readers acknowledge that the author does not render legal, financial, medical, or professional advice. The content within this book has been derived from various sources. Please consult a licensed professional before attempting any techniques outlined in this book.

By reading this document, the reader agrees that under no circumstances is the author responsible for any direct or indirect losses incurred as a result of the use of the information contained within this document, including, but not limited to, errors, omissions, or inaccuracies.

CONTENTS

Introduction   7

PART ONE
YOUR DIGITAL WAKE

1. Charting Your Digital Course   11
2. Privacy Settings and Personal Boundaries Online   15
3. The Dos and Don'ts of Sharing on Social Media   19
4. Understanding the Consequences of Online Actions   23
5. Navigating the Complexity of Online Friendships   27
6. Dealing with Digital Drama Gracefully   33
7. Cyberbullying: Prevention and Response   39
8. Digital Empathy: Understanding Emotions Online   45
9. Managing Screen Time for a Balanced Life   51
10. The Role of Parents in Digital Education   55

PART TWO
SPEAKING UP WITHOUT STEPPING ON

11. Assertiveness vs. Aggressiveness: Knowing the Difference   63
12. Techniques for Confident Communication   69
13. Setting and Respecting Boundaries   75
14. Saying No: A Skill for Life   81
15. Handling Criticism without Losing Your Cool   85
16. Advocating for Yourself in School and Beyond   91
17. Role-Playing Scenarios for Practice   97
18. Role-Playing Scenarios for Practice   103
19. Assertiveness in Group Projects and Teamwork   109
20. Parents as Role Models for Assertive Behavior   115

PART THREE
WALKING IN SOMEONE ELSE'S SHOES

21. Understanding Emotional Intelligence (EI)   123
22. Listening Skills for Deeper Understanding   129
23. The Importance of Tone in Text and Email   135

24. Supporting Friends through Digital Challenges	141
25. Empathy in Diverse Online Communities	147
26. From Trolling to Empathy: Changing Online Culture	153
27. Empathetic Responses to Online Conflicts	159
28. The Impact of Empathy on Mental Health	165
29. Building Empathy through Volunteering and Social Action	171
30. Encouraging Empathetic Conversations at Home	179

PART FOUR
SOLVING DISPUTES CONSTRUCTIVELY

31. Identifying the Root Causes of Conflicts	187
32. Communication Strategies for Conflict Resolution	193
33. The Role of Compromise in Solving Disagreements	199
34. Cool Waters: Chilling Out When Conversations Heat Up	205
35. Apologizing and Forgiving: Steps toward Healing	211
36. Charting a Course through Teen Conflicts: The Art of Mediation	217
37. Resolving Conflicts without Adult Intervention	223
38. Navigating through Stormy Seas: Lessons from the Helm	229
39. Preventing Conflicts through Proactive Communication	235
40. Creating a Conflict Resolution Plan for School	241

PART FIVE
STANDING STRONG: THE ROOTS OF SELF-ESTEEM

41. Foundation of Self-Worth	247
42. Positive Self-Talk for a Confident Self-Image	251
43. Peer Pressure: Recognizing and Resisting	257
44. The Influence of Social Media on Self-Esteem	263
45. Role Models and Mentors: Finding Your Path	269
Conclusion	275
References	277

To all the teens navigating the vibrant and sometimes tumultuous social seas:

This book is for you—the dreamers, the thinkers, and everyone in between. As you sail through these waters, may you find the courage to be authentically you. Remember, fitting in isn't about changing your colors to match the horizon but about finding where your unique spectrum is celebrated. Here's to discovering your tribe, learning the ropes, and steering your own course with confidence and kindness.

With hope and belief in your journey,

Jordan

INTRODUCTION

In the lightning-paced world of snaps, likes, and shares, mastering social skills is like navigating a massive ocean on a skateboard for both us teens and our folks. Just think about it: most of us are stuck feeling like we need to be online all the time, riding the wild waves of keeping up with our friends and not missing out on anything. It's a balancing act, trying to stay upright in the choppy waters of online chatter while meeting everyone's expectations without wiping out.

This scenario is like a giant flare, signaling to families everywhere that it's time to get serious about building real-life connections, even as our digital world keeps stretching like an endless sea.

So, here's the deal: this book is your personal surf guide, empowering you to ride the digital and face-to-face waves with equal coolness. It's packed with tricks on how to stay afloat in the sea of digital drama, express your own ideas without stepping on toes, and truly understand others—all while you're navigating the complex waters of growing up.

Crafted for both teens and parents, this guide bridges the gap between hitting 'like' and liking someone in the real world. It's divided into five killer sections, each addressing a significant aspect of the social skills puzzle, from comprehending the digital world to enhancing your real-world vibe.

By the time you finish reading, you'll be equipped with practical tools to communicate better, understand yourself more deeply, and handle peer pressure. You'll also have the know-how to create an online presence that reflects your true self. The goal is for you to step off this journey with enhanced social skills, ready to embrace the digital age with confidence and respect.

Consider this intro your ticket to an exciting adventure. Get ready to dive in, explore new ideas, and challenge yourself. Each concept is a chance to level up your social skills and enhance your connections with others. Remember, 'The strength of our relationships determines the strength of our life.' So, let's ride the waves together, learn new strategies, and create unforgettable memories. Welcome to your guide to becoming a social ninja, both online and offline. Let's embark on this thrilling journey.

PART ONE
YOUR DIGITAL WAKE

In a world where scrolling through screens and hanging out in real life blend together, the splash we make online is just as massive as the one we make when we're chilling with friends face-to-face. Like the trail a ship leaves in the water, our digital footprint can race ahead of us, setting the scene for the tales people spin about who we are. This hits extra hard for us teens as we sail our way through figuring out ourselves, all while a whole online crew is watching every move.

CHAPTER 1
CHARTING YOUR DIGITAL COURSE

When you hit 'post,' 'comment,' or 'upload,' you're not just throwing something into the digital universe. It's more like leaving a footprint in wet cement: once it's there, it's pretty hard to get rid of. The internet remembers everything, which is both cool and scary. It means you can show the world who you are, what you're proud of, and what you stand for. But, it also means that one wrong move can stick around and show up at the worst times—like when applying to colleges or looking for a job.

Getting the hang of this digital world means understanding how things work online, especially the fact that nothing ever disappears. Unlike saying something out loud that fades away, whatever you post online can stick around. It's there, ready to be found and shared repeatedly, sometimes without you even saying okay. That means a post you regret could pop back up years later, messing with your chances at a scholarship, a dream job, or even just keeping your personal life running smoothly.

So, building a positive online image isn't just about posting your wins or what you're into. It's about ensuring what you share aligns with who you are and where you see yourself going. It's about thinking long-term and choosing what to share based on how it adds to your story, which you want everyone to know.

Social media gives us some tools to help control who sees what we share, like privacy settings. Getting to know and use these settings is super important. They're like your personal filters, letting you decide who gets a glimpse into your life. Use these to make intelligent choices, not just about what to share but who you share it with. Knowing how to use these tools puts you in the driver's seat, helping you navigate the online world in a way that's safe and feels right to you.

And remember, what we do online doesn't just affect us. It spreads out, touching our friends, family, and even people we don't know. A nice comment can make someone's day, while a shared accomplishment motivates and inspires. On the flip side, something thoughtless or mean can really hurt. This connectedness is a big part of being online. It means understanding that our clicks, comments, and shares can shape our world and those around us. Being mindful of this helps us be better digital citizens, making the online space better for everyone.

In this digital era, the impressions we make online are just as impactful as the ones we make in person. What we share, the privacy settings we choose, and understanding the ripple effect of our digital footprint are vital to creating an online image that truly shows who we are and who we want to be. As we navigate this digital landscape, doing so with purpose, thoughtfulness, and a sense of responsibility can ensure that the first impression we make online is one we're proud of.

Ask the Captain

Captain, what if I post something I regret?

It's all about damage control. Review your posts regularly and clean up anything that doesn't represent you well. The internet can be forgiving if you manage your presence wisely.

How do I know what's safe to share online?

Think of each post as a piece of your story. If it's something you'd be okay with the whole world seeing, and it feels true to you, then it's safe to share.

Can what I do online really affect my future?

Yep, it can. Just like in the real world, your online actions can open or close doors to new opportunities. Ensure you're creating a digital footprint you'll be proud of as you age.

THE CAPTAIN'S GUIDING LIGHT

(Key Chapter Takeaways)

1. **Digital Footprints: Permanent Marks:** Everything you post online is like leaving a footprint in wet cement. Once it's there, it's hard to erase, so post with care.
2. **Digital Permanence: Navigational Necessity**: Realize that what goes online, stays online. Understanding this permanence helps you steer through the digital world more wisely.
3. **Authentic Online Image: True Reflection**: Your online persona should mirror your real self and aspirations. Craft an online presence you'd be proud to show both now and in the future.
4. **Privacy Settings: Control Your Course**: Mastering privacy settings on social platforms lets you manage who can view your digital journey, offering a layer of protection and personal control.
5. **Online Behavior: Ripple Effect**: Your online actions can impact you and your wider network. Aim to contribute positively to the digital community.

CHAPTER 2
PRIVACY SETTINGS AND PERSONAL BOUNDARIES ONLINE

Every click, post, and share leaves behind a digital trail in the endless ocean of the internet. Knowing how to use the tools at our disposal, like the privacy settings on social media, is crucial. These settings are the compass and map that help us decide who will journey with us, see, and interact with our shared moments. Each social media platform, from Instagram to TikTok, has its own toolkit. For instance, on Instagram, you can set your profile to private, meaning only approved followers can see your posts. On TikTok, you can control who can comment on your videos. These tools allow you to control who sees your adventures and stories.

But using these settings isn't a "set it and forget it" deal. It's more like adjusting your sails as the wind changes. As social media platforms update and change, checking back on your settings ensures your digital ship sails as privately as you want. However, remember that the sea of the internet can be unpredictable. Even the tightest privacy settings can't always prevent someone from capturing and sharing your moments without permission. If this happens, you can report the content to the platform, ask the person to remove it, or even seek legal advice.

So, before you share something, it's worth pausing on the deck and thinking about the future. Asking yourself if you'd be okay with what you're about to share being seen by anyone, even years from now, helps steer you in the right direction. It's also about respecting others' privacy, like asking for permission before sharing photos or stories that include them. This respect builds a digital world that's not just safe but kind and considerate.

Understanding these privacy settings and respecting personal boundaries online is like learning to navigate the high seas with respect and care. It's essential for creating a supportive and positive digital world, especially for teens stepping into the vast, interconnected world of online socializing.

Ask the Captain

How often should I check my privacy settings?

Checking the weather before setting sail, reviewing your settings regularly, or whenever a social media platform announces updates is wise. Stay in command of your digital journey.

Is anything ever truly private online?

Even the calmest seas can hide surprises. Assuming that anyone could see anything will guide you to share wisely and think ahead.

How can I respect others' privacy online?

Always seek permission before sharing content that includes others. It's like asking a shipmate before charting a course—they should agree to the journey.

THE CAPTAIN'S GUIDING LIGHT

(Key Chapter Takeaways)

1. **Privacy Tools: Your Digital Compass**: Privacy settings on social platforms are your navigational tools, letting you control who shares in your digital voyage.
2. **Constant Vigilance: Adjusting the Sails**: Regularly check and adjust your settings to keep your personal boundaries as you wish, adapting to changes in the social media winds.
3. **The Illusion of Privacy: Navigable Waters**: Be mindful that despite tight privacy settings, the seas are unpredictable—what you share can still spread beyond intended horizons.
4. **Pause and Reflect: Charting the Course**: Before sharing, pause to consider the long voyage of your content. Aim for decisions that will weather well over time.
5. **Respect and Consent: Sailing with Care**: Practice mutual respect in the digital realm by seeking consent before sharing content involving others, fostering a safer and kinder online community.

CHAPTER 3
THE DOS AND DON'TS OF SHARING ON SOCIAL MEDIA

Navigating the waves of social media brings opportunities and responsibilities, especially for teens stepping boldly into this dynamic landscape. It's not just about charting a path through the digital world; it's about understanding how every post, like, and comment can ripple through our online communities. The essence of sharing on social media intertwines with the art of positive contribution and mindfulness, creating a harmonious balance between expression and respect for personal and communal boundaries.

POSITIVE SHARING: SPARKING WAVES OF INSPIRATION

In the bustling realm of social media, our shares have the power to either uplift spirits or cast shadows. Positive sharing transcends the mere avoidance of negativity; it's a deliberate choice to spread content that enriches and empowers. Imagine the impact of a post celebrating a personal milestone used not just as a boast but as a beacon encouraging others to chase their dreams or a call to action for a cause close to your heart, rallying support from your digital crew. This positive current has the potential to foster a digital environment brimming with motivation, solidarity, and kindness.

NAVIGATING THE PERILS OF OVERSHARING

The boundary between sharing and oversharing can become foggy as we sail the social media seas. Oversharing or divulging too much personal information can lead to consequences ranging from minor embarrassment to severe exposure. Steering clear of these choppy waters requires mindfulness—taking a moment to ponder the value and impact of our shares. It's about asking ourselves if a post is a treasure worth sharing or is better kept hidden in our personal vault. This thoughtful pause is a compass guiding us toward sharing content that aligns with our voyage and safeguarding our digital legacy from future storms.

THE IMPACT OF OUR DIGITAL COMPASS

The content we launch into the social media ocean does more than merely float; it has the potential to set the tone for our and others' digital journeys. Uplifting content can be a lighthouse guiding toward favorable shores. In contrast, negative shares might drag the mood down into the depths. Recognizing the broad reach of our digital footprint encourages us to curate shares that mirror our values and ambitions as well as consider the emotional waves they create within our online community.

PERMISSION TO SHARE: RESPECTING THE CREW

In the vast expanse of social media, it's crucial to remember that we're part of a larger crew. Sharing content that includes fellow voyagers calls for their consent. This practice goes beyond mere etiquette; it acknowledges their right to navigate their digital presence. Whether it's a photo from a group adventure or a shared personal moment, seeking permission ensures that respect and trust remain the cornerstone of our online interactions, reinforcing the fabric of digital integrity.

By embracing these guiding principles—positively contributing to our digital community, navigating the fine line between sharing and oversharing, understanding the emotional ripples our content creates, and respecting the digital autonomy of others—we can cultivate a social media landscape that is not only safe but also nurturing and enriching for everyone involved.

Ask the Captain

What's the best way to decide what to share online?

Picture your post as a message in a bottle. Is it something you'd want the whole ocean to discover? If it's personal or you need clarification, maybe it's not ready to set sail.

Can sharing positive stories really make a difference?

Definitely. Just as calm seas make for pleasant journeys, positive posts create waves of goodwill and encouragement, making the digital world brighter.

How important is it to get permission before sharing others' moments?

It's crucial. Imagine if someone chose your course without asking. Getting permission respects everyone's right to chart their own digital path.

THE CAPTAIN'S GUIDING LIGHT

(Key Chapter Takeaways)

1. **Cultivate Positivity**: Share content that uplifts, inspiring a tide of positive energy in your digital circle.
2. **Bring Mindfulness Onboard**: Reflect on the value and potential future impact of what you share to avoid the pitfalls of oversharing.
3. **Consider the Ripple Effect**: Be aware of how your posts affect the mood and perceptions of your broader online community.
4. **Permission is Paramount**: Always seek consent before sharing content that includes others, navigating with respect and integrity.
5. **Chart a Positive Course**: By mindfully sharing and respecting personal boundaries, we can all contribute to a more supportive and enriching digital world.

CHAPTER 4
UNDERSTANDING THE CONSEQUENCES OF ONLINE ACTIONS

The digital realm is like a vast ocean, where every action creates ripples that travel far beyond the initial splash. In this interconnected space, understanding the breadth of your digital footprint is akin to recognizing how deeply those ripples penetrate the water's surface. Every post shared, every comment made, and every photo uploaded contributes to a digital footprint that paints a picture of who you are. This digital legacy, the sum of all your online actions, is not just about what is posted but also about the actions taken online - from the websites visited to the comments left on forums. These actions collectively form a permanent record that can be accessed by friends, families, potential employers, and even strangers long into the future.

The lasting nature of our online footprint means actions today can echo into our future, shaping our relationships and career opportunities. The consequences of a split-second decision to share something impulsively can spread far and wide, impacting more than just the next day's conversations. Similarly, the way we engage in online discussions—especially heated debates—can stain our reputation if not handled with care and respect for all viewpoints.

One of the darkest waters of the digital sea is cyberbullying. This modern form of harassment can have profound and lasting effects, causing distress and even leading to dire consequences. Fighting against cyberbullying isn't just about not starting it; it's also about not fueling the fire with shares, likes, or silence. Standing up against cyberbullying means promoting kindness and respect online, supporting those in the crosshairs, and reporting harmful behavior to the proper channels.

Our online behavior also sails close to legal shores. Certain actions, like sharing copyrighted content without permission, harassment, or participating in cyberbullying, can bring about legal storms, from fines to more severe consequences. It's crucial to navigate the digital realm with ethical compasses and within legal boundaries, ensuring our online journey respects personal and legal guidelines.

Yet, the digital universe isn't all about navigating through storms. It offers a horizon of possibilities for positive impact and personal growth. The internet is a treasure trove for learning, connecting with like-minded communities, and sharing inspiring stories. It's a platform where voices advocating for change can amplify their cause, from environmental conservation to social justice, demonstrating the power of digital platforms to drive significant societal shifts.

To sail these digital seas wisely, we must balance our journey with awareness of our actions' consequences, actively stand against cyberbullying, adhere to the laws of the digital realm, and seize opportunities to make a positive impact. Every online choice contributes to our digital legacy and the broader digital ecosystem. By navigating with intention and mindfulness, we can ensure that the legacy we leave is one of positive ripples, shaping a better digital world for ourselves and future generations.

Ask the Captain

How do my online actions affect my future?

Just like a ship's log, your online actions can tell a story about you to the world. Think of each action as a chapter in your digital story—make sure it's one you'd be proud to share.

What can I do to combat cyberbullying?

Be an ally on the digital seas. Support those who are targeted, speak up against bullying, and report negative behavior. Your voice can steer the ship toward kinder waters.

How can I use the internet to make a positive impact?

Use your digital presence like a beacon of light. Share stories that inspire, join causes you believe in, and use your platform to spread positivity and change.

THE CAPTAIN'S GUIDING LIGHT

(Key Chapter Takeaways)

1. **Digital Footprint: Charting Your Legacy:** Every online action contributes to your digital footprint, painting a picture of you for the future.
2. **Consequences Echo: Shaping Tomorrow:** Today's digital choices can influence your relationships and opportunities down the line. Navigate wisely.
3. **Stand against Cyberbullying: Navigating Kindness:** Combat cyberbullying by promoting respect and supporting those affected. Your actions can turn the tide.
4. **Legal Reefs: Sailing Safely:** Understand the legal implications of online actions to avoid unnecessary trouble on your digital voyage.
5. **Positive Impact: Steering Change:** Harness the power of digital platforms to inspire, educate, and advocate for causes that drive positive change in the world.

CHAPTER 5
NAVIGATING THE COMPLEXITY OF ONLINE FRIENDSHIPS

In our digital age, the map of friendship has expanded into the virtual realm, introducing us to new territories of connection and camaraderie. Online friendships, blossoming across social media, gaming platforms, and forums, bring a fresh set of navigational tools for interaction, absent the physical cues we rely on in face-to-face encounters. This shift doesn't diminish their value; instead, it highlights the importance of genuine connections and the human stories that flourish behind each screen.

CHARTING ONLINE FRIENDSHIPS

While lacking in physical presence, these digital bonds are anchored in the same principles of support, companionship, and shared experiences as their offline counterparts. Navigating these relationships requires a keen sense of communication adapted to a world where expressions and emotions are conveyed through pixels and text. Recognizing the real person on the other side of the screen is crucial for these friendships to sail smoothly in the vast ocean of digital interaction.

THE ANCHORAGE OF FACE-TO-FACE CONNECTIONS

As vast as the digital sea may be, it can't replicate the depth found in the harbors of face-to-face interaction. The tactile experiences of real-world connections—the warmth of a smile, the comfort of a presence—remain unmatched. Striking a balance between our online explorations and the physical world ensures a well-rounded social journey, enriching our ability to empathize, understand, and connect on a deeper level.

NAVIGATING DIGITAL DISPUTES

In online friendships, storms can arise in the form of conflicts, often magnified by the absence of non-verbal cues and the ease of misinterpretation. Steering through these turbulent waters requires patience, clarity, and an effort to understand the perspectives of our fellow digital navigators. Strategies such as pausing before replying, using "I" statements to express feelings, and seeking mutual resolutions can help calm the seas and preserve the integrity of our online connections.

FOSTERING DIGITAL EMPATHY

The heart of maintaining and deepening online friendships lies in cultivating digital empathy. This form of empathy bridges the gap between the virtual and the real, enabling us to connect genuinely with others despite the digital divide. Active listening, supportive gestures, respecting diverse viewpoints, and spreading positivity create a nurturing online environment where friendships can thrive.

Navigating the complexities of online friendships involves:

- Understanding the unique dynamics of these relationships.
- Balancing them with offline interactions.
- Resolving conflicts with grace.
- Fostering a culture of empathy.

By embracing these guiding principles, we can ensure that our digital connections are meaningful additions to our social circles and enriching experiences that mirror the depth and richness of in-person friendships.

Ask the Captain

How can I make my online friendships feel more real?

Dive deeper into conversations, share experiences, and plan virtual activities together. The more you invest in understanding and connecting with your digital crew, the stronger those bonds will become.

What's the best way to handle a misunderstanding online?

Anchor yourself in patience. Clarify your intentions, ask about theirs, and navigate the conversation with empathy and openness. Sometimes, a simple "I'm sorry" can mend nets and keep your friendship sailing smoothly.

How can I be more empathetic online?

Listen with the intent to understand, not just to reply. Acknowledge the other person's feelings, offer support, and remember that a kind word can be a lighthouse in someone's stormy day.

THE CAPTAIN'S GUIDING LIGHT

(Key Chapter Takeaways)

1. **Treasure Digital Bonds**: Recognize the value and authenticity of online friendships. They're real connections in a digital sea, filled with potential for support and companionship.
2. **Seek Physical Shores**: Balance your digital voyages with face-to-face interactions. The richest experiences often come from the world beyond our screens.
3. **Calm the Digital Waters**: Approach conflicts with a mindset to understand and resolve. Clear communication is your compass in navigating misunderstandings.
4. **Cultivate Empathy**: Practice empathy in your online interactions. It's the beacon that guides deeper connections and understanding in the digital world.
5. **Balance Your Sails**: Embrace the unique dynamics of online friendships while enriching them with real-world

interactions, fostering a fulfilling social journey across all horizons.

CHAPTER 6
DEALING WITH DIGITAL DRAMA GRACEFULLY

Navigating the digital seas inevitably brings us into the turbulent waters of online drama, where the currents of heated debates and conflicts can swiftly turn a calm voyage into a stormy journey. Recognizing the early signs of these brewing storms is crucial for navigating them wisely and maintaining a course that avoids contributing to chaos.

SPOTTING THE SIGNS OF DIGITAL DRAMA

Online drama can escalate quickly, transforming a simple difference of opinion into a storm of conflict. Signs of approaching drama include aggressive posting patterns, indirect swipes at individuals, and an increasing number of crewmembers joining the fray, often polarizing the discussion. When the conversation shifts from constructive to personal attacks, it's clear that it's time to batten down the hatches and consider your next moves carefully.

SAILING ABOVE THE TURMOIL

Keeping your cool amid digital squalls is vital. This doesn't mean charging into the fray but rather choosing a path that keeps the peace. Here are some strategies for staying composed:

- **Pause and Reflect**: Take a moment to step back and consider the broader implications of getting involved in the drama. A rushed response can fan the flames.
- **Anchor in Facts**: Avoid escalating the conflict by clinging to the solid ground of factual information rather than the shifting sands of opinions.
- **Consult Your Compass**: Sometimes, seeking the perspective of a trusted friend can provide the guidance needed to navigate through the drama without worsening it.

By employing these tactics, you can avoid the tempest of online drama, safeguard your digital well-being, and serve as a beacon of positivity for others.

CHARTING A COURSE TO RESOLUTION

Finding a peaceful resolution to digital disputes is paramount. Initiating private dialogue with those involved can pave the way for more constructive exchanges away from the public eye. Approaching these conversations with openness, a readiness to listen, and an understanding of the other party's viewpoint can illuminate a path to mutual agreement. Steps towards resolution include:

- **Communicate Clearly**: Share your perspective calmly and clearly, underlining your commitment to finding a solution.
- **Show Empathy**: Acknowledge the emotions and viewpoints of others, validating their experiences as part of the process.
- **Navigate Towards Compromise**: Propose solutions or compromises that consider the needs and concerns of all parties.

This method calms the storm and fosters a more respectful and supportive digital community.

LEARNING FROM THE VOYAGE

Each encounter with digital drama, while challenging, is ripe with lessons. Reflecting on these experiences sheds light on better strategies for future navigation, improving our online communication skills and resilience.

Questions to guide this reflection might include:

- What currents led to the conflict?
- How did my initial reaction influence the course of events?
- Which strategies proved effective in seeking resolution, and which did not?
- What insights have I gained for handling future digital interactions?

Viewing digital drama through the lens of a learning opportunity equips us with valuable navigational skills, enriching our journey through the digital world and contributing to a more harmonious online community. By mastering these skills, we not only navigate our digital voyages with greater ease but also contribute to calmer seas for all who sail them.

Ask the Captain

How can I tell if an online disagreement is turning into drama?

Watch for changing tides like a sudden increase in posting frequency, more aggressive language, or others joining in and taking sides. These signs indicate rough waters ahead, signaling it's time to navigate with caution.

What's the best way to keep my cool in the middle of an online storm?

Anchor yourself in calmness. Take a step back to breathe and reflect before you respond. Remember, not every provocation requires your sail; sometimes, the wisest action is to steer clear of the storm.

How do I approach resolving an online conflict?

Directly but gently. Reach out privately to discuss the matter. Enter the conversation with an open mind and a willingness to listen, aiming to find common ground and to agree to sail in peace, if not in agreement.

THE CAPTAIN'S GUIDING LIGHT

(Key Chapter Takeaways)

1. **Spotting the Storms**: Be vigilant for signs of escalating online drama, such as aggressive communication or an increasing number of participants. Recognizing these signs early helps in steering clear of potential conflicts.
2. **Maintaining Your Course**: Stay composed amidst digital squabbles by pausing to reflect, anchoring your responses in facts, and seeking guidance when needed. Your calmness can serve as a lighthouse, guiding others through foggy situations.
3. **Charting Towards Resolution**: Approach resolutions with an open heart and mind. Initiating private conversations focused on understanding and compromise can dissipate tensions and foster a supportive online atmosphere.
4. **Learning from the Journey**: Treat every instance of digital drama as a navigational lesson. Reflect on the origins of the conflict, your response, and the outcome to refine your online interaction strategies.
5. **Promoting Peaceful Waters**: By practicing patience, empathy, and clear communication, you contribute to a more positive and respectful digital environment, making the online world a safer harbor for all.

CHAPTER 7
CYBERBULLYING: PREVENTION AND RESPONSE

In the vast expanse of the digital ocean, cyberbullying represents a treacherous undercurrent capable of causing significant harm. This modern scourge, manifesting through tactics like public shaming, harassment, and spreading rumors, casts long shadows over the potential for positive connection and online learning.

SPOTTING THE SHADOWS OF CYBERBULLYING

To navigate these waters safely, one must be adept at recognizing the signs of cyberbullying:

- Repeated aggressive messages.
- Public posts designed to shame.
- Exclusion from digital communities.
- The malicious sharing of personal information.

The toll on those targeted can be severe, leading to distress and isolation. For guardians of the digital realm—parents, educators, and peers—being vigilant and informed is crucial for offering a lifeline to those caught in these turbulent waters.

SETTING SAIL WITH PREVENTATIVE MEASURES

Fortifying our digital domain against cyberbullying begins with education. Instilling values of empathy and responsibility in the digital sphere, urging thoughtful interaction, and promoting awareness of the enduring impact of online actions are pivotal. Key strategies include:

- **Navigating Privacy**: Teach and practice adjusting privacy settings to secure personal information and control who can interact with you online.
- **Mindful Sharing**: Foster a culture of mindfulness, encouraging thoughtful consideration before sharing, commenting, or forwarding content.
- **Understanding Digital Footprints**: Emphasize the permanence of online actions to encourage a responsible and positive digital presence.

Incorporating digital citizenship programs within educational and community settings can empower individuals to sail these digital waters confidently and respectfully.

RESPONDING TO THE STORM

When cyberbullying breaches the deck, a swift, calculated response is essential. Documenting the abuse forms the first line of defense, providing evidence for necessary actions. Ensuring open channels of communication helps those affected to feel supported and understood. Essential actions include:

- **Avoiding Engagement**: Guide those targeted to avoid responding directly to cyberbullies to avoid escalation.
- **Utilizing Digital Defenses**: Employ platform tools to report abusive content and block harassers, safeguarding personal digital space.
- **Securing Support**: Encourage seeking out trusted adults and professionals who can offer support and guidance through turbulent times.
- **Consulting Legal Navigators**: Seeking legal counsel is a critical step in serious cases of cyberbullying, such as ones involving threats or illegal content sharing.

Schools and communities hold significant power in creating safe harbors with clear policies and support systems for navigating and neutralizing cyberbullying incidents.

BUILDING A SUPPORTIVE FLEET

Recovery from cyberbullying requires a strong support network that offers a safe haven for those affected to rebuild and heal. Schools and communities can cultivate this environment by:

- **Launching Peer Support Groups**: Create safe spaces for sharing experiences and strategies guided by empathetic facilitators.
- **Conducting Educational Expeditions**: Host workshops to enlighten the community about cyberbullying and its eradication.

- **Deploying Mental Health Lifelines**: Ensure access to professional counseling and support for navigating the emotional aftermath of cyberbullying.

Promoting a culture of openness and respect, both in the digital and physical realms, encourages those impacted by cyberbullying to seek help while empowering witnesses to defend and support their peers. Together, we can transform the digital world into a sea of positive exchanges and growth, where the dark waves of cyberbullying are met with united resistance, compassion, and action.

Ask the Captain

How can I help someone navigating through cyberbullying?

Offer a steady compass by listening, providing support, and guiding them to use reporting tools or seek help from trusted adults. Your solidarity can be their anchor.

What's the best way to avoid cyberbullies?

Chart a course that keeps personal information private, think critically about who you interact with online, and anchor yourself in communities that promote respect and kindness.

How can I contribute to a safer digital environment?

Be a beacon of positivity; share kindly, report negativity, and support peers in distress. Your actions can inspire calmer seas for everyone.

THE CAPTAIN'S GUIDING LIGHT

(Key Chapter Takeaways)

1. **Vigilance against Shadows**: Learn to recognize the signs of cyberbullying and understand its serious impact on individuals.
2. **Fortifying Digital Shores**: Educate on and practice ethical online behavior, emphasizing empathy and the lasting impact of digital interactions.
3. **Navigating through Storms**: Respond to cyberbullying with documentation, support, and appropriate use of digital tools and legal resources.
4. **Assembling a Supportive Crew**: Foster a network of support that includes peers, professionals, and online communities, offering a safe harbor for those affected.
5. **Cultivating Calmer Waters**: Advocate for and contribute to a digital landscape marked by respect.

CHAPTER 8
DIGITAL EMPATHY: UNDERSTANDING EMOTIONS ONLINE

The digital universe, devoid of the physical cues like smiles and tones that guide our interpretations in face-to-face interactions, demands a refined skill set for understanding and conveying emotions. This chapter delves into the art of digital empathy, offering navigational aids for fostering genuine connections in a sea of pixels and text.

DECIPHERING DIGITAL CUES

Emotional cues can easily be lost or misunderstood in texts and tweets. To "read between the lines" is to tune into the nuances of language, punctuation, and even the timing of digital communications. A message's tone might hinge on something as subtle as a period or an emoji, guiding us in sensing the emotions and intentions behind the screen.

- **Contextual Compass**: The broader conversation and your history with the communicator are your maps in understanding ambiguous messages.

- **Clarification as a Beacon**: When the waters are murky, asking for clarity shows you navigate with care and intent.
- **Emojis as Emotional Anchors**: Thoughtfully used emojis can help anchor the tone of your message, providing a glimpse of the feelings accompanying your words.

THE WEIGHT OF WORDS

In the digital expanse, our words can either buoy others up or weigh them down. Crafting our messages with mindfulness prevents misunderstandings and ensures we wield our words in ways that uplift rather than harm.

- **Choosing Positive Phrasing**: Even in disagreement, positively framing your words can maintain a constructive course for the conversation.
- **Avoiding Absolutes**: Steering clear of absolutes keeps the dialogue open and prevents defensive barriers from rising.
- **Precision in Messaging**: Being specific can clarify your meaning, reduce the chance of misinterpretation, and foster clearer understanding.

EXTENDING A VIRTUAL HAND

The vastness of the digital landscape can sometimes amplify feelings of isolation. Being attuned to shifts in someone's digital presence and offering support can be a lifeline in their sea of online interactions.

- **Direct Messaging as a Safe Harbor**: A private check-in can be a safe cove, showing concern while respecting privacy.

DIGITAL EMPATHY: UNDERSTANDING EMOTIONS ONLINE

- **Public Displays of Support**: Positive public interactions can act as beacons of support, encouraging others to join in a chorus of kindness.
- **Navigating toward Help**: Sharing resources or suggesting professional support, when appropriate, shows you're there to help chart a course through rough waters.

PROMOTING A COMPASSIONATE DIGITAL COMMUNITY

Each interaction contributes to the culture of our digital world. By actively injecting positivity and understanding into our online engagements, we can help cultivate a community that values and practices digital empathy.

- **Setting the Course with Empathy**: Your example of kindness can inspire others, creating waves of positive change in online spaces.
- **Cultivating Respectful Spaces**: Setting clear expectations for empathetic and respectful interactions is vital for those steering online communities.
- **Celebrating Acts of Kindness**: Highlighting kindness reinforces its value, encouraging a culture where empathy and support flourish.

Fostering digital empathy is essential for deepening understanding and building genuine relationships in the digital domain, where our connections are mediated by screens. By honing our ability to interpret and convey emotions thoughtfully, asking for clarity when needed, choosing words with care, and actively supporting others, we chart a course toward a more empathetic and connected online world. When our journey is rooted in empathy and kindness, it enhances our digital interactions and mirrors the best of our collective humanity in the digital age.

Ask the Captain

How can I improve my digital empathy?

Practice active listening online by fully engaging with what others share, use emojis to express emotions clearly, and always seek to understand the context and feelings behind messages.

What should I do if I misinterpret someone's message online?

Acknowledge the misunderstanding, ask for clarification, and express your intentions to understand better. Openness and honesty pave the way to clearer communication.

How can I support a friend online who's going through a tough time?

Reach out with a private message to offer a listening ear, share positive comments on their posts, or provide resources that might help. Your presence and concern can be a guiding light during their dark times.

THE CAPTAIN'S GUIDING LIGHT

(Key Chapter Takeaways)

1. **Interpreting Digital Signals**: Enhance your ability to read the subtle cues of digital communication, from punctuation to emojis, to better understand emotions online.
2. **Mindful Messaging**: Choose your words with care, aiming to uplift and support rather than inadvertently causing harm.
3. **Offering Support**: Be attuned to changes in others' online behaviors and reach out with empathy and understanding, whether through private messages or public support.
4. **Contributing Positively**: Lead by example in creating a digital environment where empathy, kindness, and understanding prevail, making the online world a richer and more supportive space for all.
5. **Navigational Awareness in Digital Seas**: Cultivate an environment of mutual respect and understanding by being mindful of the context, actively seeking clarification when needed, and embracing the full spectrum of digital communication tools to express and interpret emotions accurately. Your awareness and adaptability can help smooth the waters of online interaction, ensuring a safer and more empathetic journey for everyone involved.

CHAPTER 9
MANAGING SCREEN TIME FOR A BALANCED LIFE

As the digital horizon stretches infinitely before us, screens have become ubiquitous companions, offering portals to knowledge, connections, and entertainment. Yet, navigating these waters without losing sight of the shore requires awareness of screen addiction's signs and a commitment to maintaining a healthy balance between digital and real-world engagements.

RECOGNIZING THE TIDES OF SCREEN ADDICTION

The lure of constant connectivity can lead to an unhealthy attachment to our devices, with symptoms ranging from the compulsion to check notifications incessantly to disrupted sleep patterns from late-night screen use. These behaviors signify a physical and emotional dependency on digital realms, often at the expense of tangible experiences and relationships.

CHARTING A COURSE FOR HEALTHY SCREEN TIME

Setting sail with healthy screen time boundaries is essential for preserving physical and mental well-being. Implementing strategies such as scheduled screen-free intervals, creating tech-free sanctuaries like a designated 'no-phone zone' in your home or a 'digital detox' weekend getaway, and utilizing digital wellness tools can help manage our virtual engagement. Furthermore, emphasizing the quality of online interactions over quantity encourages a richer, more meaningful digital voyage.

EMBARKING ON OFFLINE ADVENTURES

The quest for balance also involves rediscovering the joy of offline activities, which are any activities that do not involve screens or digital devices. Whether it's exploring the natural world, diving into hobbies, or engaging in physical activities, these experiences offer rejuvenation and perspective beyond the glow of screens. Volunteering and community involvement provide fulfillment and a sense of connection that digital interactions cannot replicate.

FOSTERING REAL-WORLD CONNECTIONS

The essence of life's most decadent moments often lies in face-to-face interactions, where the subtleties of human connection—body language, tone, and shared emotions—create lasting bonds and memories. Cultivating these real-world relationships enhances our emotional intelligence, empathy, and resilience, enriching our lives far beyond what digital communication can offer.

In navigating the digital age, the goal is not to shun technology but to integrate it into our lives in a way that amplifies rather than diminishes our real-world experiences. By setting healthy boundaries, engaging meaningfully with digital content, and investing in offline activities and relationships, we can chart a course through the digital world that celebrates the best of both realms.

Ask the Captain

How can I tell if I'm spending too much time on screens?

Monitor for signs like feeling a constant need to check your device, reduced physical activity, or sleep disturbances. Reflecting on whether screen time is enhancing your life or detracting from it can guide you to adjust your sails.

What are some effective ways to reduce screen time?

Set specific screen-free times, especially during meals and before bed. Designate tech-free zones in your home, and use apps to monitor and limit your digital consumption.

How can I make my screen time more meaningful?

Prioritize activities that add value—such as learning new skills, connecting with loved ones, or participating in discussions that inspire growth. Quality trumps quantity in the digital and real worlds alike.

THE CAPTAIN'S GUIDING LIGHT

(Key Chapter Takeaways)

1. **Recognize the Signs**: Be alert to the symptoms of screen addiction, understanding its impact on both your physical and emotional well-being.
2. **Set Boundaries**: Implement strategies for healthy screen use, including scheduled breaks and tech-free zones, to maintain balance.
3. **Seek Offline Treasures**: Explore activities beyond the screen that reconnect you with the physical world, from nature adventures to creative pursuits.
4. **Cultivate Real Connections**: Embrace face-to-face interactions for their unmatched depth and potential for emotional growth.
5. **Chart a Balanced Course**: Use technology as a tool to enrich your life, ensuring that your digital engagements enhance rather than eclipse your real-world experiences.

CHAPTER 10
THE ROLE OF PARENTS IN DIGITAL EDUCATION

In the vast and ever-changing digital landscape, parents stand as vital navigators for their teens, guiding them through complex online interactions with wisdom and foresight. The journey begins with parents practicing and demonstrating responsible digital behavior, setting the course for their adolescents to emulate.

MODELING DIGITAL WISDOM

Youth, particularly teens, closely watch and often mirror their parents' online habits. Parents who conscientiously curate their digital footprint, participate in online discussions with respect and maintain a balanced approach to screen time exemplify the principles of digital citizenship in action. This living lesson teaches teens the value of positive online engagement, grounding abstract concepts in the reality of daily life.

FOSTERING OPEN SEAS OF COMMUNICATION

The cornerstone of digital guidance is an open and regular dialogue about the digital universe's vast opportunities and potential pitfalls. Discussions can help teens navigate the choppy waters of cyberbullying, privacy breaches, and digital etiquette, aiming to create a safe harbor of trust and openness. By adopting an empathetic and nonjudgmental listening stance, parents encourage their adolescents to share their online voyages and seek guidance when they encounter rough waves.

COLLABORATIVELY SETTING THE COMPASS

Drawing the map of boundaries for online behavior and screen time is a collaborative venture. By involving teens in crafting these guidelines, parents respect their growing need for independence while instilling essential self-regulation and digital discernment skills. These agreements should evolve with the adolescent's age and digital landscape shifts, ensuring they remain relevant and respected.

CHARTING CURRENT TRENDS

To guide their adolescents effectively, parents must keep a keen eye on the digital horizon, staying informed about new platforms, trends, and the lexicon of the online world. This knowledge empowers parents to engage in meaningful conversations about digital phenomena, turning them into teachable moments about safety, peer pressure, and critical thinking.

UTILIZING NAVIGATIONAL TOOLS

Digital education tools and resources, from parental control software to educational websites, offer additional support in managing screen time and understanding online safety. Exploring these resources together can turn digital education into a joint adventure, strengthening the parent-teen connection and enhancing digital literacy.

CULTIVATING DIGITAL CREATIVITY AND CRITIQUE

Encouraging activities that build digital literacy and critical thinking, such as family discussions on media credibility or creative content creation, equip teens with the tools to discern and contribute positively to the online world. These activities teach valuable lessons and foster a responsible and creative online presence.

Parents, in their multifaceted role as role models, communicators, boundary-setters, and informed guides, play a crucial part in their adolescents' digital education. By demonstrating positive digital habits, encouraging open dialogue, setting collaborative boundaries, staying informed, and promoting digital literacy, parents prepare their teens to sail the digital sea with confidence, responsibility, and discernment. This comprehensive approach shields youth from the digital world's risks and empowers them to embrace its vast opportunities.

Ask the Captain

How can I start a conversation with my teen about their online activities?

Begin with curiosity rather than judgment. Share something interesting you encountered online and ask them if they've seen anything similar. Make it clear you're interested in their experiences and viewpoints, opening the door to deeper discussions.

What should I do if I'm unfamiliar with the latest digital trends or platforms my teen is using?

Admitting you don't know and asking your teen to teach you about the latest trends can be a powerful bonding experience. It shows respect for their knowledge and interest in their world.

How can I effectively set screen time limits without causing conflict?

Engage your child in the decision-making process. Discuss together the importance of balance and agree on screen time limits that consider both your concerns and their desires. Framing it as a mutual agreement rather than imposed rules can reduce resistance.

THE CAPTAIN'S GUIDING LIGHT

(Key Chapter Takeaways)

1. **Lead by Example**: Practice responsible digital habits to set a tangible example for your adolescent to follow.
2. **Open Channels of Communication**: Foster an environment where open, honest discussions about digital life are encouraged, creating a foundation of trust and understanding.
3. **Collaborate on Boundaries**: Set digital boundaries together, respecting your teen's growing independence while teaching self-regulation and responsibility.
4. **Stay Informed and Engaged**: Keep up with digital trends and platforms to better relate to your teen's online world and guide them through its challenges.
5. **Promote Digital Literacy and Creativity**: Encourage activities that enhance digital skills and critical thinking, preparing your teen to navigate the online world with discernment and confidence.

PART TWO
SPEAKING UP WITHOUT STEPPING ON

In a world where the line between assertiveness and aggressiveness often blurs, understanding the intricacies of assertive communication is more than just a skill—it's a necessity. It's like walking a tightrope; lean too much on one side, and you're tumbling into the pit of passivity. Sway too far the other way, and you're in the territory of aggression. Maintaining this delicate balance can determine the depth and quality of your relationships, your self-esteem, and even your career path. So, let's untangle the web of assertiveness and aggression, ensuring that when you speak, your words build bridges rather than burn them.

CHAPTER 11
ASSERTIVENESS VS. AGGRESSIVENESS: KNOWING THE DIFFERENCE

In the intricate dance of human interaction, distinguishing between assertiveness and aggressiveness is akin to discerning the subtle flavors in a complex dish. For instance, assertive communication could be compared to a firm but gentle handshake—confident, respectful, and balanced. It involves expressing oneself clearly and respectfully without encroaching on the territory of others. On the other hand, aggressiveness could be likened to a handshake that's too strong; it imposes one's views without regard for the other person, often leading to conflict and hurt.

To illustrate, an assertive statement could be, 'I understand your point, but I also have a different perspective.' In contrast, an aggressive statement might be, 'You're wrong and I'm right, end of discussion.'

NAVIGATING THE WATERS OF RELATIONSHIPS

Consider the scenario of navigating through a discussion on a divisive topic. Approaching with aggression and bulldozing over another's thoughts can leave the relationship shipwrecked. Yet, steering the conversation with assertiveness—acknowledging different viewpoints while sharing your own—can strengthen the bonds, building a bridge of mutual understanding and respect. Not communicating assertively can lead to misunderstandings, strained relationships, and missed opportunities for collaboration and growth.

REFLECTING ON YOUR COMPASS

Take a moment to reflect on recent conversations. Were there times you felt adrift, unable to voice your thoughts, or perhaps too forceful in your approach? These reflections are not a critique, but a compass, guiding you towards a more assertive communication style. Recognizing your tendencies is the first step in adjusting your sails towards more assertive communication, and with practice, you can steer your conversations towards more positive outcomes.

CHARTING A COURSE FOR BALANCE

Mastering the art of assertive communication is like harnessing the perfect wind to sail; it empowers you to navigate the seas of interaction with confidence and control. It involves standing your ground while respecting others' space. This balance, much like conquering the sea, requires practice, patience, and a commitment to personal growth, but the rewards are profound.

VISUAL AID: THE ASSERTIVENESS VS. AGGRESSIVENESS MAP

Imagine a chart plotting the course between assertiveness and aggressiveness. On one side, assertiveness is marked by landmarks like "Respects both parties" and "Seeks mutual understanding." The other side, aggressive territory, is noted for "Dominating the conversation" and "Disregarding others' views." This map offers a clear guide to navigating interactions with respect and balance.

REAL-WORLD NAVIGATION: SCENARIO ANALYSIS

Picture a situation where a team project is floundering due to uneven contributions. An aggressive approach might be confronting the poorly-contributing coworker publicly, leading to resentment and resistance. In a professional setting, this could damage team morale and hinder productivity. Choosing an assertive path, however, involves requesting a private discussion to express concerns and collaboratively seek solutions, charting a course toward constructive resolution. This approach respects the other person's dignity and can lead to a more positive and productive work environment.

INTERACTIVE COMMUNICATIONS

Assertive communication is the keel that keeps the ship of personal and professional relationships stable and on course. It fosters mutual respect, understanding, and trust, which are essential for healthy and productive relationships. As you traverse the seas of conversation and connection, remember that actual assertiveness benefits not just you but all those you encounter. With commitment and consciousness, you can master the skill of assertive expression, ensuring that every interaction is both respectful and meaningful, charting a course towards more prosperous, more rewarding relationships.

Ask the Captain

How do I handle a situation where being assertive doesn't seem to work?

Even the best navigators encounter unpredictable seas. If assertiveness doesn't yield the desired outcome, reassess the situation. Sometimes, a different approach or additional support may be needed. Remember, persistence and adaptability are as key in communication as they are in navigation.

Can I become more assertive even if I've always been passive?

Absolutely. Assertiveness, like any skill on the high seas, can be learned and refined over time. Start with small steps, such as expressing your preferences in low-stakes situations, and gradually build up to more significant conversations. With practice, your confidence and assertiveness will grow.

What's the best way to practice assertiveness daily?

Look for everyday opportunities to express your needs and opinions clearly and respectfully. Whether it's choosing a restaurant with friends or sharing ideas in a meeting, each day offers moments to practice and hone your assertiveness. Reflecting on these experiences will help steer your progress.

THE CAPTAIN'S GUIDING LIGHT

(Key Chapter Takeaways)

1. **Understand the Distinction**: Recognize the difference between assertiveness and aggressiveness. Assertiveness respects all parties involved, while aggressiveness seeks to dominate. Keeping this distinction in mind ensures you navigate interactions with respect and equality.
2. **Listen Actively**: Just as a captain attentively listens to the sea, practice active listening in your conversations. This shows respect for others' viewpoints and fosters more meaningful exchanges.
3. **Communicate Clearly**: Be clear and direct in expressing your thoughts and needs, akin to a captain issuing commands. Clear communication prevents misunderstandings and builds mutual respect.
4. **Maintain Emotional Balance**: Stay calm and composed, even when waters get choppy. Managing your emotions effectively is crucial for assertive communication, helping you respond rather than react.
5. **Set and Respect Boundaries**: Just as a ship has its defined course, establish personal boundaries and respect those of

others. Boundaries ensure that all interactions are conducted with mutual respect and understanding.

CHAPTER 12
TECHNIQUES FOR CONFIDENT COMMUNICATION

Navigating the vast seas of assertive communication demands more than just choosing the right words; it requires mastering how those words are delivered. Achieving harmony between what is said and how it's expressed ensures that your message reaches and resonates with its intended audience. Let's chart a course through the essential tools for effective communication.

VOICE MODULATION: SETTING THE TONE

Your voice is the wind that carries your message across the waters. Its tone sets the mood and influences how your words are received. To navigate conversations with skill:

- **Maintain an Even Pitch**: Avoid the rocks of a high-pitched voice, which may seem anxious or aggressive, and steer clear of the doldrums of monotone speech, which can disengage listeners. Aim for a calm, steady pitch that conveys confidence.

- **Control Volume**: A whisper might get lost in the waves while shouting creates stormy seas. A moderate volume ensures your message is heard clearly without overwhelming the listener.
- **Pace Yourself**: Racing through your message can capsize understanding, but moving too slowly might cause interest to drift away. A deliberate pace, punctuated by thoughtful pauses, makes your message more navigable.

THE POWER OF "I" STATEMENTS: CHARTING A PERSONAL COURSE

"I" statements transform potential confrontations into the sharing of personal feelings and needs explorations, minimizing defensiveness and fostering open dialogue. Construct them by:

- **Identifying Your Feelings**: Use "I feel ..." to express your emotions.
- **Explaining the Action**: Describe what action led to those feelings with "when ..."
- **Expressing Your Need**: Conclude by sharing what you need or what would help with "I need ..."

An example of an "I" statement is: "I feel frustrated when you interrupt me while I'm talking. I need you to let me finish what I'm saying before you respond."

ACTIVE LISTENING: THE COMPASS OF CONVERSATION

Active listening turns the monologue of speaking into the dialogue of communication. It involves total concentration on the speaker's words, showing engagement and empathy. Techniques include:

- **Reflective Listening**: Echo what you've heard to show understanding and to clarify points.
- **Non-Verbal Cues**: Employ nodding, eye contact, and leaning forward slightly to signal engagement.
- **Asking Open-Ended Questions**: Prompt further elaboration, demonstrating your interest and appreciation for the speaker's perspective. For example, "How did you feel when that happened?" or "What did you do next?"

BODY LANGUAGE CUES: THE SILENT COMMUNICATORS

Your body can broadcast messages just as loudly as your voice. Here's how to ensure your non-verbal cues support your assertive communication:

- **Maintain Eye Contact**: It conveys confidence and interest, though be mindful of cultural nuances where direct eye contact might be perceived differently.
- **Mind Your Posture**: An upright stance exudes self-assurance and readiness to engage.
- **Use Gestures Wisely**: Hand movements can emphasize points effectively; just be sure not to overdo it, as excessive gesturing can distract or confuse.

Mastering these techniques enriches your communication arsenal, empowering you to convey your messages clearly, respectfully, and effectively across any deck, whether in personal, professional, or public settings. With these tools, you can sail the communicative seas with confidence and grace.

Ask the Captain

How can I improve my active listening in noisy environments?

Focus on the speaker, perhaps by finding a quieter spot or using non-verbal cues to show you're engaged. Repeating key points back to the speaker can also help cut through the noise, ensuring you've caught the essence of their message.

What if my body language doesn't naturally match my words?

Practice is key. Try rehearsing in front of a mirror or recording yourself to become more aware of your body language and gradually align it with your verbal messages. Remember, awareness is the first step to change.

Can "I" statements come off as self-centered?

When used correctly, "I" statements focus on expressing your feelings and needs without blaming others. They foster clarity and respect in communication, steering the conversation away from conflict and towards understanding.

THE CAPTAIN'S GUIDING LIGHT

(Key Chapter Takeaways)

1. **Voice Modulation**: Your voice sets the sail for your words. Use pitch, volume, and pace to ensure your message travels smoothly and effectively.
2. **"I" Statements**: Navigate conversations with personal accountability. Expressing your feelings and needs directly can prevent misunderstandings and build stronger connections.
3. **Active Listening**: Show you're on board with the conversation. Listen attentively, reflect on what's said, and engage with genuine interest.
4. **Body Language**: Let your non-verbal cues chart a course that complements your words. Eye contact, posture, and gestures can significantly impact how your message is perceived.
5. **Embrace Continuous Learning**: The sea of communication is vast and ever-changing. Remain open to learning new strategies and refining your skills. Just as a captain continually masters the art of navigation, embrace the ongoing journey of becoming a more effective communicator with curiosity and dedication.

CHAPTER 13
SETTING AND RESPECTING BOUNDARIES

In the intricate dance of social interactions, setting and respecting personal boundaries is crucial for maintaining a healthy sense of self and fostering fulfilling relationships. These boundaries act as invisible lines that help protect our emotional well-being, time, and personal space, guiding others to interact with us respectfully and vice versa.

IDENTIFYING PERSONAL BOUNDARIES

Recognizing your own boundaries requires introspection and honesty about what you need to feel respected and secure. Key steps include:

- **Self-Awareness**: Listen to your feelings to identify when you're uncomfortable, which can indicate a needed boundary.
- **Reflection**: Analyze past situations where you felt disrespected or taken advantage of to understand what boundaries could have helped.

- **Prioritizing Needs**: Clearly define what is essential for your well-being across different areas of your life.

COMMUNICATING BOUNDARIES

Effectively conveying your boundaries to others is vital for mutual understanding and respect. Strategies for clear communication include:

- **Timing**: Choose an appropriate moment for the discussion, ideally before boundary issues arise.
- **Clarity and kindness**: Use "I" statements to explain your boundaries without assigning blame.
- **Practice**: Prepare for potential pushback by practicing your message, ensuring you can deliver it confidently and clearly.

RESPECTING OTHERS' BOUNDARIES

Honoring the boundaries set by others is just as important as establishing your own. This demonstrates empathy and respect, reinforcing positive social interactions.

- **Active Listening**: Pay close attention when others express their boundaries, seeking clarification if necessary.
- **Acknowledgment**: Verbally recognize and commit to respecting the boundaries others communicate.
- **Behavior Adjustment**: Modify your actions accordingly to consistently respect the expressed limits.

DEALING WITH BOUNDARY VIOLATIONS

When boundaries are crossed, addressing the issue assertively and constructively is essential for maintaining self-respect and healthy dynamics.

- **Reaffirm Your Boundary**: Clearly remind the person of your boundary if they disregard it.
- **Express the Impact**: Share how the violation affected you to help the other person understand the importance of your boundary.
- **Consequence Setting**: Be prepared to enforce consequences if necessary, such as reducing contact with someone who disrespects your boundaries.

TOOLS FOR NAVIGATING BOUNDARIES

- **Boundary Setting Worksheet**: A guide to help you identify, articulate, and plan for communicating your boundaries and addressing violations.
- **Role-Playing Exercises**: Practice scenarios with a partner to build confidence in asserting your boundaries in various situations.
- **Cultural Considerations**: Understand how cultural differences can impact perceptions of and approaches to boundaries, offering strategies for respectful communication across cultures.

Setting and respecting boundaries is a dynamic process of self-discovery, assertive communication, and ongoing adjustment. It's about understanding and articulating your needs, showing consideration for others' limits, and nurturing relationships where everyone's boundaries are acknowledged and valued. By actively engaging in this process, you create a foundation for respectful, fulfilling interactions that are conducive to personal growth and well-being.

Ask the Captain

How can I set boundaries without feeling guilty?

Recognize that setting boundaries is a form of self-care and respect for both yourself and others. It's about ensuring mutual respect and understanding. Guilt often stems from fear of displeasing others, but remember, your well-being is paramount and deserving of protection.

What if someone continually disrespects my boundaries?

Consistently enforce the consequences you've communicated for boundary violations. It may involve limiting interactions or seeking external support. Protecting your boundaries is crucial for your well-being.

How can I better understand someone else's boundaries?

Encourage open dialogue, ask clarifying questions, and observe their reactions in various situations. Respect and empathy are key to recognizing and honoring each other's boundaries.

THE CAPTAIN'S GUIDING LIGHT

(Key Chapter Takeaways)

1. **Chart Your Boundaries**: Understand and respect your own limits just as you would navigate a carefully mapped course.
2. **Communicate with Clarity**: Convey your boundaries assertively, ensuring your message is understood as clearly as a beacon in the night.
3. **Honor All Boundaries**: Show the same respect for others' boundaries as you desire for your own, fostering a culture of mutual respect.
4. **Navigate Violations with Strength**: Address boundary crossings with firmness and fairness, steering the relationship back to respectful waters.
5. **Embrace Learning and Flexibility**: Stay open to adjusting your boundaries as you grow and learn, navigating life's changing seas with resilience and grace.

CHAPTER 14
SAYING NO: A SKILL FOR LIFE

In the vast ocean of human interactions, the word "no" is a powerful compass guiding us toward autonomy, self-respect, and the effective stewardship of our resources. Yet, many find using this tool challenging, as saying no confidently requires practice and a deep understanding of its importance.

THE IMPORTANCE OF NO

Saying no is critical in navigating life's demands and safeguarding our time, energy, and emotional well-being. If we constantly say yes to every request, we risk overextending ourselves and neglecting our needs. Recognizing the act of saying no as a positive affirmation of self-care transforms it from a negative refusal into a significant, self-respecting decision.

OVERCOMING GUILT

Reluctance to say no often stems from guilt and fear of disappointment. To navigate these turbulent waters, it's essential to recognize and address these emotions. Reminding yourself that saying no is a declaration of self-respect, not a rejection of others, and practicing self-compassion–being kind and understanding towards yourself– are vital steps in becoming comfortable with setting boundaries.

PRACTICING REFUSAL

Saying no with grace and assertiveness is an art form that can be refined with practice:

- **Be Direct but Kind**: A clear and polite refusal respects both parties' dignity, making your stance known while acknowledging the other person' request. It's important to note that being direct doesn't mean being rude. You can say no firmly and respectfully without hurting the other person's feelings.
- **Offer a Brief Explanation**: A concise rationale for your refusal can ease the response, but beware of over-justifying your choice.
- **Suggest Alternatives**: Proposing another solution or compromise shows consideration for the relationship, even as you assert your boundaries. However, if the other person reacts negatively to your refusal, it's important to stay firm in your decision and not let their reaction sway you.
- **The Power of Choice**: At the heart of saying no is recognizing our power to choose. Each refusal is an exercise in autonomy, reaffirming our agency in deciding how we engage with the world. Embracing this power

enriches our lives with authenticity and intention, honoring our worth and the precious nature of our resources.

Mastering the skill of saying no is a journey of self-discovery and empowerment. It's about acknowledging our boundaries, respecting our values–the guiding principles that define us–and making conscious choices that align with our deepest priorities and values. As we grow in our ability to say no, we cultivate a life of balance, authenticity, and respect for ourselves and others, staying true to what truly matters to us.

Ask the Captain

How can I say no without hurting someone's feelings?

Approach the situation with empathy, expressing appreciation for the request before firmly but kindly stating your refusal. Remember, saying no isn't about rejecting the person but prioritizing your well-being.

What if I feel pressured to say yes?

Stand firm in your decision. Practice grounding yourself in your reasons for saying no, and remember that your time and energy are valuable and worth protecting.

How can I become more comfortable with saying no?

Start with small, low-stakes situations to build your confidence. Reflect on each experience to understand your feelings and reactions, gradually increasing the complexity of the scenarios as you become more comfortable.

THE CAPTAIN'S GUIDING LIGHT

(Key Chapter Takeaways)

1. **Recognize Its Value**: Understand that saying no is an essential tool for preserving your time, energy, and emotional well-being.
2. **Address Underlying Guilt**: Confront feelings of guilt by affirming your right to set boundaries and practicing self-compassion.
3. **Refine Your Technique**: Develop your ability to refuse requests gracefully, using clarity, kindness, and, when appropriate, brief explanations.
4. **Embrace Your Autonomy**: Celebrate each instance of saying no as an exercise in choice and self-determination, reinforcing your agency over your life's direction.

CHAPTER 15
HANDLING CRITICISM WITHOUT LOSING YOUR COOL

Criticism, whether delivered with the intent to guide or grieve, acts as a mirror reflecting our actions and words back at us. However, the reflection we perceive is often colored by our emotions, leading to reactions that can either foster growth or ferment grievances.

DISTINGUISHING CONSTRUCTIVE FROM DESTRUCTIVE CRITICISM

The first step towards managing criticism effectively is learning to sift through the feedback to identify its nature and intent.

- **Source and Intent:** Consider who the criticism is coming from and their potential motivation. Feedback from a trusted mentor with your best interests at heart carries a different weight than comments from someone with whom you share a competitive relationship.
- **Content and Delivery:** Constructive criticism is generally specific, aimed at actions rather than character, and delivered respectfully. Destructive criticism often targets

the person, not the behavior, and is laced with contempt rather than concern.

Understanding these differences allows us to filter feedback, retaining what is useful and discarding what is not.

RESPONDING TO CRITICISM ASSERTIVELY

Once we've identified the criticism as constructive, our response to it sets the stage for either escalation or enlightenment.

- **Pause and Process:** Before reacting, take a moment to process the feedback. This pause creates space between stimulus and response, allowing reason to guide our reaction instead of pure emotion.
- **Acknowledge and Ask:** Start by acknowledging the feedback received. This doesn't mean you agree, but it shows respect for the other person's perspective. Follow up with questions for clarification or ask for examples to better understand the specifics of the criticism.
- **Express and Engage:** Share your perspective or the context that might have been missed. This isn't about defending but about adding depth to the dialogue. Discuss ways to address the feedback, turning criticism into a collaborative effort for improvement.

This approach not only preserves relationships but also reinforces your reputation as someone open to growth and committed to excellence.

GROWTH MINDSET

Adopting a growth mindset transforms criticism from a threat into an opportunity. A growth mindset the belief that abilities and intelligence can be developed through dedication and hard work.

- **Feedback as a Gift:** View constructive criticism as a gift, an investment someone is making in your development. This perspective shifts the emotional response from defensiveness to gratitude.
- **Opportunity for Learning:** Each piece of feedback is a puzzle piece in the larger picture of personal and professional growth. Embrace it as an opportunity to learn something new about yourself or improve a skill.

This mindset makes us more receptive to feedback and fuels our journey towards becoming our best selves.

LETTING GO OF NEGATIVE CRITICISM

While constructive criticism can catalyze growth, destructive criticism requires a different strategy – release.

- **Reflect on the Source:** Sometimes, criticism says more about the critic than the recipient. Reflect on the source and its possible motivations. This can often diffuse the sting of harsh words.
- **Seek Perspective:** Share the criticism with someone you trust. They can offer a different perspective, helping you see the situation in a new light or confirming that the criticism is not worth your worry.

- **Self-Compassion:** Be kind to yourself. Remind yourself of your strengths and accomplishments. Self-compassion buffers against the negative impact of harsh words.
- **Release and Redirect:** Consciously choose to let go of negative criticism. Visualize setting it adrift or physically write it down and tear it up. Then, redirect your focus to constructive feedback and actionable goals.

Navigating the choppy waters of criticism requires a keen eye for discernment, a steady hand for assertive response, a compass oriented towards growth, and the wisdom to know when to release and redirect. It's through mastering these skills that we turn the mirror of criticism from a source of distress into a tool for development, reflecting back not just who we are but who we have the potential to become.

Ask the Captain

How can I differentiate between constructive and destructive criticism?

Pay attention to the source, intent, and content of the feedback. Constructive criticism usually comes from a place of wanting to help and focuses on specific behaviors or actions, offering ways to improve. Destructive criticism often feels personal, lacks specificity, and provides no clear direction for growth. Trust your instincts—if it feels like it's more about tearing down than building up, it may not be worth your energy.

What's the best way to respond when I receive criticism that I disagree with?

Start by acknowledging the feedback, showing you value the other person's perspective. Express your viewpoint or the context they might be missing in a calm and collected manner. If you still disagree after a respectful discussion, suggest finding a compromise or a third perspective to help bridge the gap. Remember, the goal isn't to win an argument but to foster understanding and growth.

How do I let go of negative criticism that's affecting my self-esteem?

Reflect on the source and their possible motives—often, it's more about them than you. Share your feelings with a trusted friend or mentor who can offer a different perspective. Practice self-compassion, reminding yourself of your strengths and achievements. If the criticism lingers in your mind, visualize releasing it or write it down and physically discard it. Focus on constructive feedback and your personal growth journey.

THE CAPTAIN'S GUIDING LIGHT:

(Key Chapter Takeaways)

1. **Constructive Channels**: Always seek to filter criticism through the lens of growth and improvement. Constructive criticism is a lighthouse guiding you toward better shores, while destructive feedback is a fog to navigate with caution.
2. **Steady as She Goes**: In the face of criticism, maintain your composure. Let the calm sea of your self-worth and confidence guide you, using criticism as a tool for growth rather than a wave that tosses you.
3. **Dialogue Anchors**: Use open, respectful communication as your anchor in responding to criticism. Acknowledging feedback and expressing your perspective fosters dialogue and mutual understanding, preventing misunderstandings from turning into storms.
4. **Sails of Self-Compassion**: When navigating the rough waters of criticism, hoist the sails of self-compassion. Remind yourself of your journey, strengths, and the unique value you bring to the table. Self-kindness is the wind that propels you forward.
5. **Crew of Support**: Remember, you're not sailing alone. A trusted crew of friends, family, and mentors can provide the support and perspective needed to navigate through criticism. Their encouragement and advice can help you steer through even the toughest feedback.

CHAPTER 16
ADVOCATING FOR YOURSELF IN SCHOOL AND BEYOND

Navigating the waters of educational settings and the workplace demands a clear understanding of one's needs and the skill to communicate these needs effectively. From the bustling halls of academia to the dynamic arenas of professional life, the art of self-advocacy stands as a beacon, guiding individuals toward realizing their full potential. This skill, rooted in assertive communication, paves the way for achieving mutually beneficial outcomes and building networks of support that bolster one's journey toward personal and professional fulfillment.

SELF-ADVOCACY IN EDUCATIONAL SETTINGS

In the education landscape, self-advocacy is crucial. It's about understanding your needs, preparing your case, choosing the right moment, and using clear, assertive language. These steps empower students to take charge of their educational experience and communicate their needs effectively.

- **Identify Your Needs:** Begin by pinpointing exactly what you need to enhance your learning experience. Is it extra time for tests, a quiet study area, or access to additional resources?
- **Prepare Your Case:** Arm yourself with information to support your request. This might include understanding school policies, gathering evidence of your needs, and anticipating potential questions.
- **Choose the Right Moment:** Timing can significantly impact the outcome of your conversation. Opt for a moment when your teacher or advisor can give you their full attention.
- **Use Clear, Assertive Language:** Express your needs confidently and precisely, avoiding ambiguous language. Focus on how the support will help you achieve your educational goals.

ASSERTIVENESS IN THE WORKPLACE

The leap from the educational realm to the vast expanse of the workplace introduces new challenges and opportunities for self-advocacy. Here, asserting oneself can influence career trajectories, shape professional relationships, and ensure a fulfilling work environment. Whether negotiating salaries, voicing ideas in meetings, or seeking feedback for growth, assertiveness is vital. To navigate these waters:

- **Acknowledge Your Value:** Recognize the skills and perspectives you bring. Self-awareness is the foundation of confidence.

- **Articulate Your Achievements and Aspirations:** Be ready to discuss your accomplishments and how they align with your career goals. This clarity can guide conversations about promotions, projects, or professional development opportunities.
- **Practice Active Listening:** Engage fully in discussions, showing genuine interest in others' viewpoints. This not only fosters mutual respect but also shows that you value their input. It positions you as a collaborative and assertive team member, making others feel heard and appreciated.
- **Seek Feedback Proactively:** Ask for input on your performance regularly. This demonstrates a commitment to growth and opens channels for constructive dialogue.

NEGOTIATION SKILLS

At the heart of assertive communication is negotiation. It's a skill that goes beyond personal interactions and finds relevance in every aspect of life. Negotiation is about finding common ground and solutions that honor the interests of all parties involved, making it a crucial part of self-advocacy.

- **Prepare Thoroughly:** Understanding your needs and those of the other party can illuminate areas of common ground and potential compromise.
- **Communicate Clearly and Respectfully:** Present your perspective and listen to the other party with an open mind. Aim for dialogue that explores solutions rather than debates positions.
- **Stay Focused on the Goal:** Keep the conversation directed toward the desired outcome, avoiding detours into unrelated or emotionally charged territory.

- **Be Willing to Compromise:** Sometimes, the ideal solution involves give and take. Be prepared to adjust your requests while still meeting your core needs.

BUILDING A SUPPORT NETWORK

The journey of assertiveness does not unfold in isolation. Surrounding oneself with mentors, peers, and allies who champion your growth and support your endeavors is not just beneficial, it's crucial. This network serves as a sounding board, offering advice, encouragement, and perspectives that enrich your understanding and approach. To cultivate this community:

- **Seek Mentors Who Inspire You:** Identify individuals in your field of study, workplace, or broader professional network whose qualities and achievements resonate with you. Reach out to them for guidance and mentorship.
- **Engage with Peers Who Share Your Aspirations:** Join forums, professional associations, or study groups that align with your interests. These spaces can provide support, collaboration opportunities, and a sense of belonging.
- **Nurture Reciprocal Relationships:** Invest time and energy in supporting others' goals. A strong network is built on mutual respect and shared support.

In the grand scheme of personal and professional development, the ability to advocate for oneself stands as a cornerstone, underpinning a structure of success and satisfaction. Whether navigating the intricacies of educational settings, asserting oneself in the professional realm, honing negotiation skills, or building a support network, the essence of self-advocacy permeates every endeavor. Through assertiveness, individuals can view and interact with the world as passive observers and active participants, shaping their destinies with clarity, confidence, and purpose.

Ask the Captain

How can I become more effective in expressing my needs in educational settings?

Start by clearly identifying your needs and gathering any necessary information or evidence to support your requests. Practice expressing these needs in a concise and specific manner, and choose a suitable time to discuss them with educators or advisors.

What strategies can I use to enhance my assertiveness in professional negotiations?

Preparation is key. Understand your own needs and those of your counterpart, aiming to find common ground. Approach the negotiation with clear, respectful communication, and be open to compromise to achieve a mutually satisfactory outcome.

How can I build a supportive network that encourages my professional growth?

Seek out mentors who inspire you and engage with peers who share your aspirations. Participate in professional forums or groups relevant to your interests. Remember, a supportive network is based on give-and-take—be ready to offer your support to others as well.

THE CAPTAIN'S GUIDING LIGHT

(Key Chapter Takeaways)

1. **Recognize Your Compass**: Understand and value your unique contributions and needs in both educational and professional settings.
2. **Prepare for Your Voyage**: Arm yourself with knowledge and evidence to support your advocacy efforts, ensuring you can navigate conversations with confidence.
3. **Communicate with Clarity**: Use assertive communication to articulate your needs and goals, fostering an environment of mutual respect and understanding.
4. **Master the Art of Negotiation**: Approach negotiations with preparation, respect, and a willingness to find collaborative solutions.
5. **Cultivate Your Crew**: Build and maintain a network of mentors, peers, and allies who support and enrich your personal and professional development journey.

CHAPTER 17
ROLE-PLAYING SCENARIOS FOR PRACTICE

In the realm of communication, our bodies often speak louder than our words. Body language is the undercurrent of our interactions, conveying confidence, sincerity, and respect without a whisper. Mastering the subtle art of non-verbal cues strengthens assertive communication. It ensures a symphony between our spoken words and the messages our bodies send.

NON-VERBAL ASSERTIVENESS

Assertive body language encompasses a spectrum of physical expressions that amplify our message of self-assurance and respect when aligned with our words.

- **Posture**: An upright, open stance transforms us into a pillar of confidence. In contrast, a slouched or closed posture may convey uncertainty or disinterest.
- **Eye Contact**: The bridge of engagement, maintaining appropriate eye contact, signals you are present and value the interaction.

- **Facial Expressions**: A calm, composed demeanor communicates control, whereas genuine smiles can diffuse tension and foster connection.

Incorporating these elements into your communicative repertoire enhances the resonance of your assertiveness, allowing your physical presence to underscore your verbal intent.

INTERPRETING BODY LANGUAGE

Reading the non-verbal cues of others is just as vital, offering insights into their emotional state and engagement. Observing these cues enables you to tailor your approach, ensuring the communication remains open and assertive.

- **Responses to Your Cues**: An open response to your assertiveness suggests a positive reception; closed body language may indicate a need to adjust your approach.
- **Signs of Discomfort**: Identifying discomfort or disagreement through crossed arms or lack of eye contact can signal a moment to reassess your strategy.
- **Engagement Indicators**: Positive affirmations such as nods or smiles encourage the flow of assertive dialogue, signaling agreement and understanding.

Attuning to these signals guides communication dynamics, maintaining a balance of assertiveness and receptivity.

HARMONY OF VERBAL AND NON-VERBAL COMMUNICATION

The true potency of communication lies in the harmony between what we say and how our bodies speak. This congruence fortifies the authenticity and impact of our messages.

- **Consistency**: Aligning your non-verbal cues with your verbal messages solidifies your communication, reinforcing your intent and sincerity.
- **Adaptive Feedback**: Using the non-verbal feedback of others as a compass can help you navigate and realign your communication strategies for clearer understanding.

Achieving this alignment clarifies your messages and cements trust and credibility in your interactions.

CULTIVATING ASSERTIVE BODY LANGUAGE

Developing an assertive presence is a journey of mindful practice and reflection.

- **Mirror Practice**: Use a mirror to observe and adjust your posture, expressions, and gestures, aiming for a demeanor that projects confidence and openness.
- **Record and Review**: Recording practice conversations can reveal discrepancies between verbal and nonverbal communication and offer insights for improvement.
- **Real-Time Adjustments**: Stay aware of your body language in daily interactions and make immediate adjustments to ensure it supports your assertive goals.

- **Feedback Loop**: Solicit and utilize feedback from peers on your non-verbal cues, integrating their insights into your continuous development.

By dedicating time to refine your body language, you craft a persona that naturally exudes assertiveness, enriching your interactions with a silent-yet-powerful dialogue of confidence and respect.

Ask the Captain

How can I maintain assertive body language even when I'm feeling nervous?

Anchor yourself in practices that boost confidence, such as deep breathing or visualizing a successful interaction before it begins. Remember, your body language can influence your emotions just as your emotions can affect your posture and gestures. By adopting assertive body language, you may begin to feel more confident as well.

What's the most important aspect of body language when trying to assert myself?

While all aspects of body language contribute to the message you're conveying, maintaining appropriate eye contact is often the keel that keeps your ship steady. It communicates confidence and engagement, key components of assertive communication.

How can I get better at reading others' body language in conversations?

Practice is your compass here. Pay deliberate attention to others' non-verbal cues during interactions. Over time, you'll start to notice patterns and better understand what different cues might mean. Reflecting on these observations after conversations can also sharpen your interpretive skills.

THE CAPTAIN'S GUIDING LIGHT

(Key Chapter Takeaways)

1. **Steady Your Stance**: Just like a sturdy ship braves the waves, a strong, open posture communicates confidence and readiness to engage. Stand or sit straight, with shoulders back and open to signal self-assurance and interest in the conversation.
2. **Eyes on the Horizon**: Eye contact is the lighthouse guiding the way in communication, illuminating sincerity and engagement. Maintain appropriate eye contact to show you are fully present in the interaction.
3. **Calm Seas Ahead**: A composed facial expression and controlled gestures are like calm waters, indicating that you're in control of the situation and respectful of the

ongoing conversation. Let your face reflect your genuine interest and your gestures underscore your points without overwhelming your words.

4. **Navigating through Feedback**: Use the non-verbal feedback you receive as a map to guide the conversation. If you notice signs of discomfort or disagreement, consider adjusting your approach to maintain open and productive dialogue.
5. **Practice Makes Perfect**: Like mastering the seas, developing assertive body language takes practice. Engage in exercises that enhance your awareness and control of your non-verbal cues, and seek feedback to fine-tune your skills.

CHAPTER 18
ROLE-PLAYING SCENARIOS FOR PRACTICE

Role-playing is a dynamic rehearsal space, offering a unique opportunity to refine our assertive communication skills in a risk-free environment. This method allows us to practice navigating potential real-world situations, adjusting our sails as we learn to handle different reactions gracefully and confidently.

THE VALUE OF PRACTICE

Just as a musician dedicates hours to practice before a performance, mastering assertive communication requires repetition and rehearsal. Role-playing bridges the gap between theoretical knowledge and practical application, transforming our understanding of assertiveness into actionable skills.

SCENARIO SELECTION

Choosing realistic scenarios that mirror potential challenges in various aspects of life is key to effective role-playing. These scenarios range from professional negotiations and setting personal boundaries to discussing household responsibilities. Selecting situations that stretch our comfort zones prepares us to navigate similar challenges assertively in real life.

FEEDBACK AND REFLECTION

The cycle of action, feedback, and reflection is crucial in role-playing, offering insights into our performance and highlighting areas for improvement.

- **Feedback Session**: After each role-play, engage in a feedback session that values honesty and specificity, which are instrumental in identifying areas for growth.
- **Reflect on Feedback**: Contemplate the feedback, considering what struck a chord and any surprises. This reflection is vital in integrating the lessons learned.
- **Adjust and Repeat**: Apply the feedback to future role-plays, fine-tuning your approach and gradually enhancing your assertive communication skills.

This iterative process is the cornerstone of becoming more effective, assertive communicators.

BUILDING CONFIDENCE THROUGH REPETITION

Confidence in assertive communication grows with each role-playing session as we explore various strategies and witness their impact.

- **Gradual Escalation**: Begin with less daunting scenarios, slowly advancing to more complex challenges as your confidence solidifies.

- **Celebrate Progress**: Acknowledge every step forward, however small, recognizing your growth and the practical application of new strategies.
- **Consistent Practice**: Maintain a regular role-playing routine to keep your assertive communication skills sharp and ready for real-life application.

Through consistent practice, feedback, and reflection, role-playing nurtures a deep-rooted confidence in our ability to communicate assertively. This preparation ensures we're not only ready to face challenging conversations but are also adept navigators of the rich and complex seas of human interaction.

Ask the Captain

How can I find partners willing to engage in role-playing exercises with me?

Look within your circle of trusted friends, family, or colleagues who also wish to improve their communication skills. You can also join public speaking groups or workshops that offer role-playing as part of their training.

What should I do if I find myself reacting defensively during a role-play?

Use it as a learning opportunity. Discuss your reaction with your role-playing partner to understand triggers and experiment with different responses. Reflecting on these moments can be incredibly valuable for personal growth.

Can role-playing actually make a difference in real-life situations?

Absolutely. Role-playing is a rehearsal for reality, allowing you to experiment with and refine your responses in a safe environment. It builds muscle memory for assertive communication, making you more prepared and confident when similar situations arise in real life.

THE CAPTAIN'S GUIDING LIGHT

(Key Chapter Takeaways)

1. **Choose Realistic Scenarios**: Engage in role-plays that mirror actual challenges you face or anticipate, providing practical experience in navigating these situations assertively.
2. **Embrace the Feedback Loop**: Value honest, specific feedback from role-playing partners, reflecting on it to fine-tune your assertive communication strategies.
3. **Practice Builds Confidence**: Regular role-playing strengthens your assertive communication "muscles," boosting your confidence to handle real-life challenges effectively.

4. **Celebrate Your Voyage**: Recognize and celebrate each step of progress made through role-playing, acknowledging your growing ability to communicate assertively.
5. **Expand Your Crew**: Seek role-playing partners who share your commitment to growth, creating a supportive network that fosters mutual learning and improvement.

CHAPTER 19
ASSERTIVENESS IN GROUP PROJECTS AND TEAMWORK

Navigating the collaborative waters of group projects and teamwork in educational and professional settings requires a captain's mastery of assertive communication. This skill is the rudder that ensures clear expression of ideas, smooth sailing through group dynamics, effective conflict resolution, and leadership that inspires collective effort and respect.

EXPRESSING OPINIONS CLEARLY

Straightforward and assertive expression of ideas is like setting a course for a successful voyage, especially when working with a group. Here's how to ensure your voice is heard and respected in group discussions:

- **Prepare Your Map**: Organize your thoughts and plan your contributions ahead of time. A well-prepared mind is like a charted course, purposefully guiding the discussion.

- **Begin with Affirmation**: Positively acknowledging others' ideas sets a collaborative tone, like a friendly flag signaling cooperation.
- **Be Specific**: Using specific examples to support your points is like using landmarks for navigation, making your arguments more persuasive and understandable.
- **Seek the Crew's Input**: Inviting feedback opens the deck for a richer exchange of ideas, fostering mutual respect and collaboration.

NAVIGATING GROUP DYNAMICS

A ship's crew comes from diverse backgrounds, each contributing unique strengths. Ensuring your assertive voice contributes positively involves:

- **Understanding the Crew**: Recognize the communication styles and dynamics of your team. Like knowing the sea, this awareness guides your interactions.
- **Flexibility in Communication**: Adapting your approach to fit the situation and team members is akin to adjusting sails to the wind, making your interactions more effective.
- **Making Space on Deck**: Encourage quieter members to voice their ideas, enriching the team's discussions and ensuring all voices are heard.

CONFLICT RESOLUTION

Conflicts are the storms of teamwork. Handling them with assertive and constructive communication can lead to clearer skies and stronger bonds:

- **Address Storms Early**: Confront conflicts when they arise, preventing them from growing into hurricanes.
- **Focus on the Horizon, Not the Waves**: Concentrate on behaviors and outcomes, not personal attributes, to keep discussions objective and focused on solutions.
- **Find Safe Harbor in Compromise**: Look for solutions that respect everyone's fundamental needs, navigating towards a consensus that all can accept.
- **Listen to the Wind**: Practice active listening to understand all perspectives, a crucial step in navigating towards resolution.

LEADERSHIP AND ASSERTIVENESS

Assertive communication underpins effective leadership in group settings, guiding the team toward common goals with clarity and mutual respect:

- **Be the Compass**: Model assertive behavior, demonstrating how to engage respectfully and productively in discussions and conflict resolution.
- **Empower Your Crew**: Allow team members to take the helm in their areas of responsibility, boosting their confidence and commitment to the project's success.
- **Chart the Course**: Provide clear directions and constructive feedback, ensuring the team remains aligned

with project goals and navigates challenges effectively.
- **Encourage a Cohesive Culture**: Foster an environment where open communication, respect, and collaborative problem-solving are the norm, enhancing team performance and satisfaction.

In the collaborative journey of group projects and teamwork, assertiveness is the key to unlocking a treasure chest of productive interactions, innovative solutions, and meaningful professional relationships. By mastering the art of assertive communication, you contribute effectively to the team's goals and chart a course for personal growth and leadership development.

Ask the Captain

How can I assert myself in a group without coming across as overbearing?

Find the balance by being clear and concise in your communication, showing appreciation for others' contributions, and actively listening. Just like a captain needs both authority and empathy, blend your assertiveness with respect for the team's input.

What's the best way to handle a team member who dominates discussions?

Address it by affirming the value of diverse input and suggesting structured turn-taking or specific times for each person to share ideas. Like navigating through narrow straits, guide the conversation with gentle but firm control.

How do I deal with conflict in a team setting without causing more tension?

Approach conflict like seeking calm waters after a storm—focus on the issue, not the person, and seek a solution that considers everyone's core concerns. Encourage open dialogue and use active listening to understand all sides.

THE CAPTAIN'S GUIDING LIGHT

(Key Chapter Takeaways)

1. **Preparation and Planning:** Like charting a course before setting sail, organize your thoughts and contributions ahead of team discussions. A well-prepared mind guides effective communication.
2. **Positive Framing:** Begin your input with acknowledgment of existing ideas, like a lighthouse guiding ships safely to shore, setting a constructive tone for your contributions.
3. **Encourage All Voices:** Ensure every crew member has a chance to speak, like a captain who values the input of every sailor, enriching the team's journey with diverse perspectives.
4. **Resolve Conflicts Constructively:** Navigate through team conflicts with a focus on solutions and mutual respect, steering the team back to collaborative waters.

5. **Lead with Assertiveness and Empathy:** Combine clear, confident leadership with understanding and support, guiding your team towards its goals while fostering a positive and productive environment.

CHAPTER 20
PARENTS AS ROLE MODELS FOR ASSERTIVE BEHAVIOR

In the symphony of family life, parents lead the orchestra, setting the rhythm and tone for their teens' understanding of assertive communication through their actions' subtle-yet-profound language. Teens learn to harmonize self-expression with respect for others within the framework of daily life.

MODELING ASSERTIVENESS

Parents have the stage to model assertiveness in every interaction, demonstrating that one's needs can be voiced clearly and respectfully without silencing others. Observing a parent handle a disagreement with poise and respect serves as a live lesson in self-advocacy for adolescents, teaching them the nuances of assertive communication in real time.

TEACHING THROUGH EXAMPLE

Life's canvas is rich with moments for parents to illustrate assertiveness. They share personal stories of self-advocacy in various situations. These narratives help teens see assertiveness as a relatable and essential aspect of interaction, encouraging them to embrace their own voices.

ENCOURAGING ASSERTIVE COMMUNICATION

Creating an environment that champions adolescents' confidence to speak up requires active encouragement and practice:

- **Role-playing scenarios** provide a rehearsal space for teens to try out assertive responses with parents as their supportive audience.
- **Positive reinforcement** for assertive communication by teens reinforces the value of such interactions.
- **Guided reflection** on different approaches to situations enhances teens' ability to navigate future interactions assertively.

This nurturing approach cultivates a view of assertiveness as both positive and practical.

OPEN FAMILY COMMUNICATION

At the heart of teaching assertiveness is creating a family culture that promotes open dialogue, where every member can share freely and feel valued. Regular family meetings become the stage for practicing assertiveness, guided by parental empathy and the mutual exchange of thoughts and feelings.

This open communication ethos ensures that family life becomes a foundation upon which youth build their capacity to interact assertively beyond the home, ready to face the world's complexities confidently.

By conducting the family orchestra with assertiveness, parents impart lessons that resonate beyond words, shaping their teens' ability to navigate life's dynamics with respect for self and others. This legacy of assertiveness, rooted in parents' everyday actions and guidance, prepares adolescents for a future of meaningful and respectful relationships.

Ask the Captain

How can I model assertiveness for my teens when I struggle with it myself?

Start with small steps, celebrating your successes along the way. Share your journey with your teens, showing them that learning assertiveness is a process that requires practice and patience. Your efforts to improve can inspire them to embrace their own assertive path.

What if my adolescent is too shy to practice assertiveness even in role-plays?

Encourage them by starting with scenarios where they feel most comfortable, perhaps using characters or stories they like. Gradually introduce more realistic scenarios as their confidence grows, always ensuring a supportive and positive environment.

How can we maintain open communication in our family when everyone is so busy?

Set aside a regular time each week for family meetings, making them a priority. Use this time to connect, share experiences, and practice open, assertive communication. Showing that family time is important can help make these meetings a cherished part of your routine.

THE CAPTAIN'S GUIDING LIGHT

(Key Chapter Takeaways)

1. **Lead by Example**: Demonstrate assertive communication in your daily interactions, providing a living example for your teens to emulate.
2. **Share Your Stories**: Use personal experiences as teachable moments to illustrate the value and methods of assertive behavior in relatable ways.
3. **Encourage Voice and Choice**: Support your teens in expressing their opinions and making choices, reinforcing the importance of their voices within the family and beyond.
4. **Cultivate an Open Forum**: Establish your home as a place of open dialogue, where each family member can

practice assertiveness in a supportive environment.
5. **Embrace the Journey Together**: Recognize that learning to communicate assertively is a shared journey, one that involves growth, challenges, and triumphs for both parents and teens.

PART THREE
WALKING IN SOMEONE ELSE'S SHOES

Imagine you're at a bustling coffee shop, trying to order your favorite drink amidst the chaos of peak hour. Under the pressure of back-to-back orders, the barista mixes up your order. Now, you could react in frustration, or you could pause, recognize their stress, and respond with understanding. Your choice at that moment hinges on a crucial skill: emotional intelligence (EI). EI enables us to navigate daily interactions with empathy, patience, and insight. It's the difference between a day filled with conflicts and one where we foster connections and understanding, even in challenging situations.

EI is often the unsung hero in tales of personal and professional success. It's the force that guides us to respond to situations and people with a balanced blend of heart and mind. From the classroom to the boardroom, understanding and managing our emotions and recognizing and influencing the feelings of others can transform how we interact with the world.

CHAPTER 21
UNDERSTANDING EMOTIONAL INTELLIGENCE (EI)

Emotional intelligence (EI) is a term that refers to the ability to recognize, understand, and manage our own emotions, as well as the ability to recognize, understand, and influence the emotions of others. At its core, EI is about awareness and control. It's recognizing when you're getting impatient in a long line, understanding why that is, and deciding how to respond in a productive, not destructive, way. But it's also about sensing frustration in others before it bubbles over, helping to steer situations towards positive outcomes.

COMPONENTS OF EI

EI comprises four main elements:

- **Self-Awareness:** This is about knowing your emotions, strengths, weaknesses, and triggers, such as understanding that you're not a morning person and that your mood can be a bit rough around the edges before your first coffee.

- **Self-Management:** Here, we're discussing controlling or redirecting your disruptive emotions. It's about thinking before you act. It's choosing to take a deep breath and count to ten when irritated.
- **Social Awareness:** This element involves empathy, understanding others' emotions, and picking up on social cues. It's noticing when a friend is quieter than usual and might need a chat.
- **Relationship Management:** This is about making your interactions positive. It involves clear communication, effective conflict handling, and the art of making people feel valued.

EI AND EMPATHY

Empathy is the vital bridge between our emotional world and that of others. It's the ability to step into someone else's shoes, to truly feel what they're feeling. EI lays the foundation for empathy, enabling you to connect with people on a deeper, more meaningful level. This connection has the power to transform a potential argument into a constructive conversation, a group of individuals into a cohesive team, and an ordinary day into one filled with enriching interactions.

DEVELOPING YOUR EI

Improving your EI is a journey that requires time and effort, but it's a journey you can embark on with confidence. Here are some practical strategies and exercises to kickstart your EI development:

- **Keep a Mood Diary:** Track your emotions and what triggers them. Over time, you'll start to see patterns. You may always be irritable after skipping breakfast, or certain people may drain your energy.
- **Practice Pausing:** Before reacting in any situation, take a moment. This pause lets you choose how to respond rather than just reacting on autopilot.
- **Ask for Feedback:** Sometimes, it's hard to see ourselves clearly. Asking trusted friends or family how you come across in different situations can offer valuable insights.
- **Empathy Exercises:** Imagine how others might feel in various situations. If you see someone upset, think about what might be going through their mind. This practice helps to develop your empathy muscles.

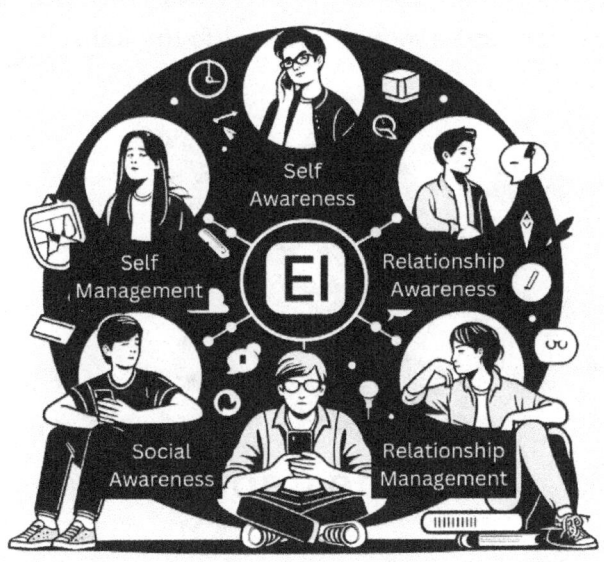

Textual Element: Daily EI Practices Checklist

Here is a checklist for daily practices to enhance each EI component could serve as a practical tool for personal development. I suggest spending five minutes reflecting on your day and emotions for self-awareness. For self-management, identify stress-relief techniques that work for you. In fostering social awareness, the checklist could encourage active listening during conversations. Lastly, relationship management might suggest practicing expressing appreciation for others daily.

By improving your emotional intelligence, you're enhancing your understanding and empathy and transforming your perceptions and interactions with the world around you. It's about creating a life where every interaction is enriched with understanding, empathy, and effective communication. Developing your EI equips you with the tools to navigate the intricacies of human emotions, leading to deeper connections and a more fulfilling life for yourself.

Ask the Captain

How can I improve my self-awareness if I'm not used to reflecting on my emotions?

Begin by setting aside a few minutes each day to reflect on your experiences and how they made you feel, almost like a captain logs the day's journey. Use prompts if needed, such as "What moment today made me happiest?" or "When did I feel challenged?" This daily practice can sharpen your emotional awareness over time.

Can emotional intelligence help me with stress at work?

Absolutely. By enhancing your self-management skills, you can learn to recognize stress signals early and employ strategies to navigate through them, similar to how a skilled sailor uses techniques to weather a storm. Techniques like deep breathing, prioritizing tasks, or seeking support can mitigate stress's impact.

How do I practice empathy without taking on everyone else's emotional baggage?

Empathy involves understanding and sharing the feelings of others, not carrying them. Imagine empathy as a bridge that allows you to visit someone on their island of experience and then return to your own. Setting boundaries for yourself and practicing self-care are essential parts of maintaining this balance.

THE CAPTAIN'S GUIDING LIGHT

(Key Chapter Takeaways)

1. **Chart Your Emotional Course**: Cultivate self-awareness by regularly reflecting on your emotions and reactions. Understanding your emotional landscape is like charting a

course that guides your journey through internal and external challenges.
2. **Steady Your Emotional Sails**: Practice self-management by developing strategies to calm stormy emotions. This skill ensures you can navigate through emotional turbulence with grace, maintaining control over your reactions.
3. **Tune into Your Crew's Emotions**: Enhance your social awareness by paying attention to the emotional cues of those around you. Like a captain attuned to the crew's morale, this awareness strengthens your ability to navigate social interactions smoothly.
4. **Cultivate a Cohesive Crew**: Strengthen relationship management by fostering positive interactions and resolving conflicts with diplomacy. Effective leadership, like that of a respected captain, is built on clear communication, mutual respect, and shared goals.
5. **Empower Your Voyage with Empathy**: Practice empathy to connect deeply with others, enriching your interactions and enabling you to guide conversations and relationships toward positive outcomes. Empathy is the compass that ensures you remain oriented towards understanding and compassion in your interactions.

CHAPTER 22
LISTENING SKILLS FOR DEEPER UNDERSTANDING

In the realm of emotional intelligence, listening extends far beyond merely hearing words. It's a skill that, when finely tuned, allows us to truly understand and connect with others. This skill, active listening, is a cornerstone of empathy and a powerful tool for building meaningful relationships.

THE IMPORTANCE OF ACTIVE LISTENING

At its heart, active listening is about fully engaging with the speaker, giving them your complete attention, and making a conscious effort to understand the words, emotions, and intentions behind them. It's about validating their feelings and experiences, creating a space where they feel seen and heard. This level of attentiveness can transform conversations into opportunities for genuine connection and understanding.

BARRIERS TO EFFECTIVE LISTENING

Despite its value, active listening can be challenging to achieve. Several obstacles can hinder our ability to listen effectively:

- **Distractions:** Our world, particularly the digital one, is full of distractions that can distract our attention from the person speaking to us. Whether it's a buzzing phone or a running to-do list in our heads, these distractions make it challenging to be fully present.
- **Prejudices:** Sometimes, our biases and preconceived notions about people or topics can act as filters, warping how we interpret what's being said.
- **Emotional Reactions:** Strong emotional reactions to the discussion can disrupt active listening. We might miss the speaker's point entirely if we're too caught up in how we feel about the subject.

PRACTICING ACTIVE LISTENING

To overcome these barriers and hone our active listening skills, consider integrating the following practices into your conversations:

- **Minimize External Distractions:** Put away electronic devices, find a quiet place for meaningful conversations, and ensure you're in a comfortable setting that fosters attentiveness.
- **Check Your Biases:** Make a conscious effort to set aside your judgments and approach each conversation with an open mind.
- **Focus on the Speaker:** Use non-verbal cues like nodding and maintaining eye contact to show you're engaged.

These actions help you stay focused and communicate your interest to the speaker.
- **Reflect and Clarify:** Periodically summarize what you've heard and ask clarifying questions. This practice ensures you've understood the speaker correctly and shows them you're actively processing their words.

LISTENING BEYOND WORDS

To deepen your understanding of the speaker's message, listening to what's not being said is crucial. Non-verbal cues like tone of voice, facial expressions, and body language can provide additional layers of meaning to their words. Here are a few tips to enhance your ability to listen beyond words:

- **Pay Attention to Tone and Pacing:** Changes in the speaker's tone or speed can indicate emotions they might not express explicitly.
- **Watch for Non-Verbal Cues:** Facial expressions and gestures can explain the speaker's feelings and attitudes.
- **Notice Silences:** Pauses or breaks in the conversation can be just as telling as the words themselves. They might indicate the speaker is searching for the right words, feeling emotional, or needing a moment to collect their thoughts.

Incorporating these elements into your listening practice can significantly enrich your understanding of others, fostering deeper connections and empathy. By actively engaging in conversations, minimizing distractions, and being mindful of verbal and nonverbal cues, you'll find yourself hearing and genuinely understanding those around you.

Ask the Captain

How can I improve my focus during conversations in noisy environments?

Like focusing on a distant lighthouse through fog, concentrate on the speaker by positioning yourself to minimize background noise and using visual cues to maintain connection. Imagine the background noise fading away as you tune into the speaker's words.

What should I do if I realize my biases are influencing how I listen?

Acknowledge the current steering you off course and consciously adjust your bearings. Remind yourself to approach the conversation with curiosity and openness, seeking to discover rather than confirm.

How can I encourage others to practice active listening?

Lead by example, like a captain setting the course for the crew. Share the principles of active listening during calm waters and model this behavior in your interactions. Often, the change in one person can ripple out, influencing the listening habits of others.

THE CAPTAIN'S GUIDING LIGHT

(Key Chapter Takeaways)

1. **Set Your Course with Intent**: Approach every conversation with the deliberate intent to listen deeply, focusing fully on the speaker as if they are the stars you're navigating by.
2. **Navigate Past Distractions**: Steer clear of the modern-day sirens—our devices and internal distractions—to ensure you're fully present and attentive.
3. **Read the Emotional Currents**: Tune into the undercurrents of the conversation, observing non-verbal cues and listening to the silences, to grasp the full scope of the speaker's message.
4. **Signal Your Engagement**: Use your body language and responses to show you're actively engaged, reflecting the speaker's message to confirm understanding and offering insights where appropriate.
5. **Foster Open Waters for Dialogue**: Encourage a culture of active listening in your personal and professional circles, promoting an environment where every voice is heard and valued.

CHAPTER 23
THE IMPORTANCE OF TONE IN TEXT AND EMAIL

In the digital age, our conversations often unfold on screens, leaving behind the rich tapestry of nonverbal cues that inform face-to-face interactions. This shift to text-based communication introduces unique challenges, particularly in maintaining the intended emotional tone. Misinterpretations are not uncommon and can lead to unnecessary conflicts or misunderstandings. Recognizing the potential pitfalls of digital dialogue is the first step toward mitigating them.

CHALLENGES OF DIGITAL COMMUNICATION

The absence of voice inflection, facial expressions, and body language in text and email means that much of the message's emotional context can be lost or misconstrued. A joke might come off as sarcasm; an attempt at brevity can seem cold or indifferent. This gap between intended and received messages can skew perceptions and strain relationships.

CONVEYING TONE THROUGH TEXT

Achieving the right tone in digital communications requires clarity, empathy, and, sometimes, creativity. Here are some techniques to ensure your message is understood as intended:

- **Choose Your Words Carefully:** Words are powerful. Opt for language that clearly conveys your emotional state or intent. "I'm excited to see you!" leaves little room for misinterpretation compared to a more subdued "See you soon."
- **Structure for Emphasis:** Use paragraph breaks, bullet points, or italics to highlight key points or convey the flow of your thoughts more naturally.
- **Preface Your Tone:** A quick preface can set the right expectation if you're concerned that the message could be taken in a way you don't intend. For example, "I hope this doesn't come off as harsh, but ..."
- **Read Aloud before Sending:** Before sending your message, read it aloud to yourself. This can help you catch any potential misunderstandings and adjust the tone accordingly.

INTERPRETING TONE IN DIGITAL MESSAGES

On the flip side, being the recipient of digital messages requires a degree of open-mindedness and the benefit of the doubt. Here are tips to avoid misinterpretation:

- **Consider the Context:** If a message seems off, consider the sender's usual communication style and the current circumstances. They might be rushed or under stress.

- **Seek Clarification:** If unsure about a message's tone, asking for clarification is okay. A simple "Did you mean ..." can clear up any confusion.
- **Don't Jump to Conclusions:** Avoid making immediate assumptions about the sender's emotions or intentions. Take a moment to reflect before responding.

EMOJIS AND DIGITAL EXPRESSIONS

Emojis, GIFs, and stickers offer a playful and visually engaging way to add emotional nuance to our digital conversations. They can soften the tone, convey humor, or express feelings more vividly than words alone. However, their interpretation can vary widely based on age, culture, or familiarity with digital platforms. Here's how to use them effectively:

- **Match the Recipient's Style:** Feel free to reciprocate if the person you're communicating with often uses emojis. It shows that you're speaking their language.
- **Use Emojis for Clarity, Not Confusion:** Choose emojis that clearly support or enhance your message. A well-placed smiley face can convey warmth, while a thumbs-up can signal agreement without ambiguity.
- **Be Mindful of Overuse:** While emojis can enrich communication, overuse can dilute your message or appear unprofessional, depending on the context. Strike a balance that respects the nature of your relationship and the conversation.

Digital communication, devoid of the non-verbal cues we rely on in person, demands a heightened awareness of how our words may be received. By applying thoughtfulness and creativity to our digital interactions, we pave the way for more transparent and more empathetic exchanges. Whether through carefully chosen words, the strategic use of emojis, or simply taking a moment to seek clarity, we can navigate the challenges of digital communication with finesse, ensuring our relationships remain strong and misunderstandings are few.

Ask the Captain

How can I ensure my humor is understood in text messages?

When sailing the uncertain waters of humor in text, consider using emojis to signal your jesting tone, or clearly state your intent with phrases like "just kidding!" to ensure your humor lands as intended without misinterpretation.

What's the best approach when I receive a digital message that upsets me?

Anchor yourself before responding. Allow yourself some time to process your emotions and consider seeking clarification. Remember, the digital sea can distort messages and a calm, measured response can prevent a storm.

How can I express empathy effectively in a text or email?

To convey empathy, use language that explicitly acknowledges the other person's feelings, like "I understand how that might be frustrating." Emojis can also serve as visual aids to express empathy and warmth.

THE CAPTAIN'S GUIDING LIGHT

(Key Chapter Takeaways)

1. **Craft with Care**: Choose words that accurately reflect your intent and tone, ensuring your digital messages are clear beacons in the night.
2. **Navigate with Structure**: Use formatting as your compass, guiding the reader through your message with ease and clarity.
3. **Signal Your Intent**: Preface messages with a brief indication of tone to avoid misunderstandings, setting a clear course from the outset.
4. **Decode with Openness**: Approach received messages with an open heart and mind, steering clear of quick judgments and fostering understanding.
5. **Embark with Emojis**: Utilize emojis judiciously to add emotional nuance to your messages, ensuring they complement rather than cloud your intent.

We Would Love Your Feedback and Support

As you explore "Essential Social Skills for Teens," we trust you've discovered valuable insights and practical strategies for navigating social interactions with confidence. Your feedback is crucial for tailoring our content to best serve your needs and those of fellow readers. If you've found the book helpful, please consider sharing your thoughts by leaving a review on Amazon.

Scan the QR code below or visit the provided link to access the review page. Your support is deeply appreciated as we strive to empower teens with essential social skills.

https://www.amazon.com/review/create-review/?asin=B0D3CPYSGG

CHAPTER 24
SUPPORTING FRIENDS THROUGH DIGITAL CHALLENGES

In this digital era, where interactions often occur behind screens, it becomes crucial to recognize when a friend is facing online challenges. While the digital world offers a space for connection, it can also be a source of distress. Identifying the signs of such distress and knowing how to offer support respectfully and effectively is key to helping friends navigate the complexities of their online experiences.

RECOGNIZING DIGITAL DISTRESS

Digital distress can manifest in various ways, subtly altering a person's online behavior and communication. Signs to watch for include:

- **Changes in Online Activity:** A sudden increase or decrease in posting, commenting, or responding can indicate shifts in emotional well-being.
- **Tone of Communication:** Pay attention to any noticeable changes in the tone of your friend's digital

communications. Messages that are consistently negative or anxious signal underlying issues.
- **Withdrawal from Online Groups or Activities:** If a friend who is typically active in online communities suddenly pulls back or disengages, it might be a sign of discomfort or distress in those spaces.
- **Indirect Cues:** Sometimes, what's not said directly can hint at distress. Vague posts or social media updates that suggest unhappiness or frustration warrant a closer look.

OFFERING DIGITAL SUPPORT

When a friend struggles, reaching out in a thoughtful and supportive manner can make a significant difference. Here's how to approach this delicately:

- **Private and Direct Communication:** Initiate a private conversation through direct message or text, expressing your concern and willingness to listen. This creates a safe space for them to open up if they choose to.
- **Be Patient and Non-Judgmental:** Offer your support without pressing for details. Let them share as much or as little as they're comfortable with, and assure them of your unconditional support.
- **Share Resources:** Share resources that might help them address their challenges. This could include links to online support groups, articles, or professional help services.
- **Empathize:** Try to understand their feelings and validate their experiences. Sometimes, knowing someone else understands and cares can be incredibly comforting.

NAVIGATING DIGITAL BOUNDARIES

While offering support, respecting your friend's digital boundaries is essential. This respect ensures that your efforts to help are both appropriate and welcomed. Consider these guidelines:

- **Respect Their Privacy:** If they're not ready to discuss their issues, respect their choice. Pushing for information can cause further stress or discomfort.
- **Avoid Public Comments:** Publicly addressing your concerns for this friend on social media can put them in an uncomfortable spotlight. Keep your support private unless they've indicated otherwise.
- **Be Mindful of Advice:** Offer advice cautiously and only if they're receptive. Unsolicited advice, even with the best intentions, can sometimes feel intrusive.

ENCOURAGING OFFLINE SUPPORT

While digital support can be invaluable, encouraging friends to seek offline support can also be beneficial. Here's how to gently guide them towards additional resources:

- **Suggest Talking to Someone They Trust:** Encourage them to share their concerns with a family member, friend, or professional who can offer support and guidance.
- **Recommend a Break from Digital Spaces:** Sometimes, taking a step back from online platforms can provide much-needed relief and perspective. Suggest engaging in offline activities they enjoy or spending time in nature to decompress.

- **Offer to Accompany Them:** If they're considering seeking professional help but are hesitant, offer to accompany them to an appointment. Your presence can provide comfort and encouragement.

In today's interconnected world, where digital challenges can significantly impact well-being, being a supportive friend involves:

- Recognizing signs of distress
- Offering empathetic and respectful support
- Encouraging the exploration of offline resources

By doing so, you play a crucial role in helping your friends navigate their digital experiences more positively and healthily.

Ask the Captain

How can I approach a friend who seems to be struggling online without making them feel uncomfortable?

Approach with the same discretion and care as you would if navigating through fog. Start by expressing your general concern and availability to listen, without directly pointing out their online behavior. Let them know you're there, no matter the weather, ready to provide support when they're ready to share.

My friend's online posts have been worrying me, but they insist they're fine. What should I do?

Sometimes, the best course is to keep your ship steady and close by. Respect their response, but gently remind them of your concern and willingness to listen, offering a safe harbor whenever they might need it. Consistency in your support can be a comforting beacon for them.

How can I encourage a friend to take a break from social media if I think it's affecting their mental health?

Suggest a digital detox as if proposing an adventure to uncharted territories, perhaps even committing to join them on this journey. Highlight the potential benefits with enthusiasm, like rediscovering offline hobbies or spending more time in nature, making it a shared quest for well-being.

THE CAPTAIN'S GUIDING LIGHT

(Key Chapter Takeaways)

1. **Watch for Signals**: Stay alert to changes in your friend's digital behavior or tone, as these can be distress flares signaling their need for support.
2. **Private Channels Are Key**: Reach out through direct, private communication, creating a safe space for your friend to open up, akin to a calm cove away from the stormy sea.
3. **Offer a Compassionate Ear**: Listen with patience and empathy, validating their feelings without immediately

trying to fix their problems. Just as a steady presence can calm the seas, your understanding can offer solace.
4. **Respect Their Journey**: Understand that each person navigates their digital challenges in their own time and way. Offer your support without pushing them to share more than they're comfortable with.
5. **Guide Towards Calmer Shores**: Encourage activities and strategies that promote well-being both online and offline. Suggesting a digital break or connecting them with resources is like pointing them towards a lighthouse in the dark.

CHAPTER 25
EMPATHY IN DIVERSE ONLINE COMMUNITIES

In an era where digital platforms are the new town squares, our interactions are no longer confined by geography. The internet has knit together a rich tapestry of global voices, each contributing to a vibrant mosaic of perspectives. This digital diversity is a treasure trove of learning and growth opportunities. Still, it also brings its own set of challenges. Navigating this landscape requires a keen sense of empathy and an ability to understand and share the feelings of others, even when their experiences are worlds apart from our own.

THE POWER OF DIVERSE PERSPECTIVES

When we dive into online communities, we're not just logging into forums or social media platforms; we're stepping into a global classroom. Every post, comment, and shared story is a lesson from a different viewpoint. Engaging with this diversity broadens our understanding, challenges our preconceptions, and enriches our worldview. Through this engagement, we learn not just about the world but also about ourselves. By embracing diverse perspectives, we foster a culture of learning and openness, making our online spaces richer and more enlightening.

CHALLENGES OF DIGITAL DIVERSITY

However, this digital melting pot can also be a breeding ground for misunderstandings and conflicts. Language barriers, cultural differences, and the absence of non-verbal cues often lead to misinterpretations. A comment meant as constructive criticism might be perceived as harsh judgment. An attempt at humor can easily be misunderstood as an offense. These misunderstandings can escalate quickly, turning what could be insightful exchanges into battlegrounds of words.

BUILDING BRIDGES THROUGH EMPATHY

To navigate these waters smoothly, empathy becomes our compass. It allows us to see beyond the surface of typed words to the human experiences and emotions underneath. Here are some strategies for cultivating empathy in digital interactions:

- **Active Inquiry:** When you encounter a viewpoint that puzzles you, ask questions. Approach with curiosity, not judgment. Clarify misunderstandings and show you're genuinely interested in understanding the other person's perspective.
- **Pause before You Respond:** Reacting quickly to something that triggers you is easy. Instead, take a moment to consider the other person's context. They might be coming from a place of pain, frustration, or misunderstanding. A pause gives you the space to craft a thoughtful and empathetic response.

- **Share Your Own Experiences:** Sometimes, sharing your experiences can help bridge the gap. It means saying, "I see you, I hear you, and here's where I'm coming from." This exchange of personal stories can be a powerful tool for building empathy and understanding.

CREATING INCLUSIVE DIGITAL SPACES

Online communities' true potential lies in their inclusion, offering a platform for all voices to be heard. Creating such spaces requires a collective effort and a commitment from all members to foster empathy and understanding. Here are some tips for contributing to more inclusive digital communities:

- **Moderate with Empathy:** If you can moderate discussions, do so with empathy. Set clear guidelines for respectful interaction and step in when conversations turn disrespectful, but always aim to understand the root cause of conflicts. Sometimes, a private, empathetic conversation with involved parties can resolve issues more effectively than public moderation.
- **Amplify Diverse Voices:** Make a conscious effort to amplify voices that might be less loud or as heard. Share articles, posts, and stories from people with different backgrounds. This enriches the community and encourages a culture of learning and inclusivity.
- **Educate Yourself and Others:** Take the initiative to learn about different cultures, perspectives, and experiences. Share what you learn with your community. Education is a powerful tool against ignorance and prejudice.
- **Promote Kindness and Understanding:** Lead by example. Treat every interaction as an opportunity to

spread kindness and foster understanding. A single empathetic response can set the tone for the entire community.

With all its diversity, the digital world offers us an unprecedented opportunity to learn from each other and grow beyond the confines of our own experiences. By approaching these interactions with empathy, we enrich our lives and contribute to creating online communities that are genuinely inclusive, understanding, and united in their appreciation of human diversity.

Ask the Captain

How can I effectively communicate empathy in a heated online discussion?

Like calming a storm with words, express understanding and seek common ground. Use phrases that acknowledge the other's feelings and offer a perspective that aims to soothe, not inflame, such as "I understand where you're coming from, and I see how that could be frustrating."

What if my attempts at empathy are met with hostility in online spaces?

Sometimes, the seas remain rough despite our best efforts. If empathy is met with hostility, maintain your composure, reiterate your intent to understand, and, if necessary, disengage gracefully, preserving the peace of your own vessel.

How do I handle cultural misunderstandings in online communities?

Approach with the humility of a student eager to learn. Acknowledge the misunderstanding, ask for guidance, and express your willingness to understand better. Your openness to learning can turn the tide of conversation towards mutual respect.

THE CAPTAIN'S GUIDING LIGHT

(Key Chapter Takeaways)

1. **Chart a Course of Curiosity**: Embrace the diverse perspectives encountered online as opportunities for growth, approaching each with an open heart and mind.
2. **Anchor in Active Inquiry**: Seek to understand the vast landscapes of human experience with questions that bridge distances, inviting a confluence of stories and insights.
3. **Steer with Understanding**: In the face of digital diversity, let empathy guide your interactions, ensuring that even the simplest exchanges are imbued with respect and compassion.
4. **Illuminate with Shared Stories**: Share your journey and listen to those of others, lighting the way for connections that transcend digital boundaries.

5. **Cultivate Seas of Inclusivity**: Through empathetic actions and advocacy for diverse voices, contribute to creating online communities that are havens of understanding and respect.

CHAPTER 26
FROM TROLLING TO EMPATHY: CHANGING ONLINE CULTURE

Some individuals find a misplaced sense of empowerment in trolling through the vast expanse of the internet, where anonymity often acts as a veil. This behavior, aimed at provoking or upsetting others, not only significantly mars the digital landscape but also turns potentially enlightening spaces into arenas of distress. Understanding the motivations behind trolling and addressing it with empathy can be transformative, fostering a healthier online environment for all.

UNDERSTANDING TROLLING

Trolling is not just a random act of online malice; it's a behavior rooted in a complex web of motivations. For some, it's a pursuit of amusement at the expense of others' feelings, a misguided form of entertainment. Others might troll as a way to exert power, disrupt conversations, or challenge what they perceive as dominant narratives. Recognizing these motivations is pivotal, not to excuse the behavior but to understand its origins to address it effectively.

- **Seeking Attention:** Many trolls thrive on the reactions they provoke. Understanding this can guide our responses to them.
- **The Feeling of Anonymity:** The internet's anonymity can encourage individuals to act in ways they wouldn't in face-to-face interactions.
- **Desire to Disrupt:** Some see trolling as a way to challenge norms or provoke thought, albeit through negative means.

RESPONDING TO TROLLS WITH EMPATHY

Engaging trolls with empathy might seem counterintuitive, yet it can be a remarkably powerful strategy. Instead of perpetuating the cycle of negativity, empathetic responses can disarm the troll, demonstrating that their tactics won't elicit the desired outcome. Here are ways to implement this approach:

- **Avoid Immediate Reactions:** Pause before responding. This space allows you to approach the situation with calmness and perspective.
- **Respond Selectively:** Not all trolling warrants a response. Sometimes, ignoring the troll to deprive them of the attention they seek is best.
- **Seek Understanding:** When engaging, aim to understand their perspective. Asking questions about their viewpoints can sometimes reveal genuine concerns beneath the provocative veneer.
- **Set Boundaries:** Clearly state your willingness to engage in constructive dialogue but not in hostile exchanges. This sets a tone of respect for the conversation.

PERSONAL RESPONSIBILITY

Each of us has a crucial role in shaping online culture. Embracing personal responsibility means being acutely aware of our own contributions to digital spaces. It involves:

- **Reflecting on Our Behavior:** Regularly assess our interactions. Are we adding value and understanding, or are we contributing to negativity?
- **Educating Ourselves:** Stay informed about the impact of our words and actions online. Understanding the broader consequences can guide more responsible behavior.
- **Promoting Positive Engagement:** Lead by example. Share content that uplifts others, contributes to discussions with respect, and offers support where needed.

ADVOCATING FOR CHANGE

Going beyond individual actions, advocating for a broader cultural shift towards empathy and kindness online is not just important—it's absolutely necessary. This advocacy can take many forms, from supporting platforms that enforce respectful interactions to creating content that celebrates empathy. Strategies include:

- **Supporting Empathetic Platforms:** Patronize and promote online spaces known for their positive culture and active moderation against trolling.
- **Creating and Sharing Positive Content:** Use your online presence to spread kindness. Share stories of empathy, highlight positive interactions, and celebrate acts of understanding.

- **Engaging in Digital Activism:** Participate in or initiate campaigns to combat online negativity. This could involve raising awareness about the impacts of trolling or supporting initiatives that promote digital empathy.
- **Educating Others:** Offer guidance to friends, family, or followers about navigating online spaces with empathy. Share strategies for dealing with trolling and fostering a positive digital footprint.

In the digital age, where our online interactions can profoundly impact our real lives, steering the culture away from trolling towards empathy is not just desirable—it's necessary. By understanding the roots of harmful online behavior, responding with empathy, taking personal responsibility, and advocating for a kinder digital world, we contribute to an online culture that mirrors the best parts of humanity. This shift enriches our digital experiences and reinforces the internet as a space for growth, learning, and genuine connection.

Ask the Captain

How do I maintain my composure when encountering trolling in online discussions?

Like facing a storm at sea, maintain your course with patience and perspective. Remember, the troll seeks to disturb your peace; choose instead to navigate with the steady hand of empathy, focusing on the broader journey rather than the temporary squall.

Can empathy really change the behavior of someone who trolls?

While not every stormy heart can be calmed, empathy can indeed shift the winds. Some who troll do so from a place of misunderstanding or unmet needs; your empathy might just be the lighthouse that guides them to more peaceful waters.

How can I help foster a more empathetic online community?

Start by charting a course of kindness in your own interactions. Like the captain of a ship setting an example for their crew, your actions can inspire others. Support platforms that prioritize empathy, share content that uplifts, and engage in discussions with compassion and respect.

THE CAPTAIN'S GUIDING LIGHT

(Key Chapter Takeaways)

1. **Understand the Currents**: Recognize the complex motivations behind trolling, navigating these waters with insight and patience.
2. **Respond with a Steady Hand**: Choose empathy over escalation, steering conversations towards understanding and respect.

3. **Chart Your Own Course**: Reflect on your digital footprint, ensuring your interactions contribute positively to the vast online sea.
4. **Raise the Sails of Positivity**: Lead by example, creating waves of kindness and understanding that ripple across the digital ocean.
5. **Join Forces for a Kinder Internet**: Advocate for online spaces that champion empathy, contributing to a collective effort to transform the digital landscape into one of respect, understanding, and genuine human connection.

CHAPTER 27
EMPATHETIC RESPONSES TO ONLINE CONFLICTS

Conflicts are almost inevitable in the vast digital terrain where voices from all corners of the globe converge. However, the key to turning these conflicts from divisive to constructive lies in our ability to respond with empathy. By putting ourselves in others' shoes, we not only understand their perspectives but also pave the way for resolutions that respect the feelings and needs of all involved.

THE ROLE OF EMPATHY IN CONFLICT RESOLUTION

Empathy acts as a powerful catalyst in resolving online conflicts. It shifts the focus from winning the argument to understanding the underlying concerns and emotions driving the disagreement. This shift is crucial because when people feel understood, they are more open to finding common ground. Empathy in conflict resolution does not mean sacrificing one's stance but rather approaching the situation with a mindset that values relationship preservation alongside problem-solving.

- **Reduces Defensiveness:** Recognizing and acknowledging the other party's emotions decreases their need to defend their position vigorously, creating a more conducive environment for dialogue.
- **Fosters Mutual Respect:** Even in disagreements, approaching the conversation with empathy signals respect for the other person's perspective, laying a foundation for constructive interaction.

UNDERSTANDING THE OTHER SIDE

To navigate online conflicts with empathy, we must strive to understand the perspectives and emotions of everyone involved. This understanding can be achieved through steps designed to bridge the gap between differing viewpoints:

- **Ask Open-Ended Questions:** Encourage the other party to share more about their feelings and perspectives. Questions like "Can you help me understand why you feel that way?" invite elaboration without judgment.
- **Reflect on Their Emotions:** Paraphrase what you've understood about their feelings and perspective. This reflection ensures you've grasped their point and shows them they've been heard.
- **Acknowledge the Validity of Their Emotions:** You don't have to agree with their stance to acknowledge their feelings are valid. A simple "I see why that upset you" can go a long way in diffusing tension.

COMMUNICATING WITH EMPATHY

Expressing your viewpoint in a manner that's respectful and considerate of others' feelings is the essence of empathetic communication. This approach entails several vital practices:

- **Use "I" Statements:** Frame your responses to focus on your feelings and reactions rather than attributing blame. For example, "I feel concerned about ..." instead of "You always ..."
- **Avoid Absolutes:** Words like "always" and "never" can escalate conflicts. They paint issues in black and white, ignoring the nuances of most situations.
- **Express Understanding:** Even if you disagree, acknowledging the other person's perspective demonstrates empathy. Statements like, "I understand where you're coming from, but I see it differently because ..." help keep the conversation grounded in mutual respect.

REACHING RESOLUTION

Finding a resolution that all parties can accept is the ultimate goal of empathetic communication in conflicts. Achieving this outcome involves a deliberate and thoughtful approach:

- **Identify Common Goals:** Even in conflict, there are often shared objectives. Highlighting these can shift the interaction from adversarial to cooperative.
- **Brainstorm Together:** Invite all parties' suggestions on resolving the conflict. This collaborative approach generates more potential solutions and ensures everyone feels involved in the resolution process.

- **Agree to Disagree, Respectfully:** Sometimes, a complete agreement isn't possible. In such cases, agreeing to disagree while respecting each other's viewpoints can be a peaceful way to conclude the discussion.

Empathy in online conflicts is not about conceding or compromising your values but about engaging in a way that acknowledges and respects the humanity of all involved. By striving to understand before being understood and communicating with consideration for others' feelings, we can transform potential discord into opportunities for deeper connection and understanding.

Ask the Captain

How can I remain empathetic in heated online debates?

Like maintaining course in a gale, focus on the humanity behind each comment. Remember that behind every opinion is a person, navigating their own sea of experience. Pausing to reflect before you respond can help you reply with empathy and consideration.

What if my attempts at empathy are met with continued hostility?

Sometimes, despite our best efforts, the waters remain rough. If empathy doesn't calm the storm, it may be wise to steer away and disengage, preserving your peace and ensuring the safety of your vessel.

How can I encourage others to approach conflicts with empathy?

Lead by example, like a lighthouse guiding ships through the night. Your approach can illuminate a path for others, showing that empathy not only resolves conflicts but also builds stronger, more respectful communities.

THE CAPTAIN'S GUIDING LIGHT

(Key Chapter Takeaways)

1. **Chart a Course of Understanding**: Use empathy to navigate the underlying emotions and perspectives in conflicts, seeking to understand before being understood.
2. **Navigate with Open Questions**: Like explorers seeking new lands, use open-ended questions to discover the depth of others' experiences and viewpoints.
3. **Signal Respect and Validation**: Acknowledge and validate the feelings of others, even in disagreements, to foster an atmosphere of mutual respect.
4. **Steer Clear of Stormy Reactions**: Choose to respond rather than react. A moment of pause can change the course of an online interaction.

5. **Anchor in Common Goals**: Identifying shared objectives can help calm turbulent waters, guiding all parties towards a resolution that respects the diverse crew of the digital realm.

CHAPTER 28
THE IMPACT OF EMPATHY ON MENTAL HEALTH

Empathy, often seen as the ability to understand and share the feelings of others, plays a crucial role in our mental health and that of those around us. It acts as a bridge, allowing us to connect with others on a deeply emotional level. This connection can be a source of tremendous support and healing for both the giver and the receiver of empathy.

EMPATHY AS A SUPPORT MECHANISM

When we share our struggles with someone who responds with genuine empathy, feeling understood and not alone can be profoundly comforting. It's akin to finding a safe harbor amid a storm. The person offering empathy provides emotional support simply by acknowledging and validating the other's feelings. This validation is robust; it can transform feelings of isolation into feelings of connection and solidarity. Knowing someone truly understands can be a significant step towards healing for someone going through a tough time.

- **Reduces Isolation:** Empathy can break down the walls of loneliness, showing someone they're not alone in their experience.
- **Validates Feelings:** It acknowledges that the person's emotions are real and justified, which is crucial for emotional healing.
- **Encourages Sharing:** Knowing that one is likely to be met with empathy makes it easier to open up about complicated feelings.

THE BENEFITS OF BEING EMPATHETIC

Practicing empathy benefits those on the receiving end and also enriches the person offering it. Engaging in empathetic interactions can lead to the following:

- **Increased Connection:** Empathy fosters a more profound connection and understanding between individuals, strengthening relationships.
- **Reduced Stress:** Engaging in supportive, empathetic interactions lowers stress levels for both parties. It shifts focus away from our troubles and towards caring for others, which can be therapeutic.
- **Enhanced Emotional Intelligence:** Regularly practicing empathy can improve our ability to read and understand the emotions of others, an essential component of emotional intelligence.

EMPATHY AND SELF-CARE

While empathy is undeniably beneficial, balancing our empathetic engagements with self-care is essential. Constantly absorbing the emotional states of others can lead to empathy fatigue, a state of emotional exhaustion that can diminish our capacity to offer compassion. To maintain this balance:

- **Set Emotional Boundaries:** Recognizing when to step back and protect our emotional well-being is crucial. Knowing our limits allows us to offer empathy without overextending ourselves.
- **Engage in Self-Reflection:** Regularly check in with yourself to assess your emotional state. If you're feeling drained, it might be time to focus on self-care.
- **Practice Self-Compassion:** Be as kind and understanding to yourself as you would be to others. Acknowledge your feelings and give yourself permission to take breaks and recharge.

PROMOTING MENTAL HEALTH AWARENESS

Empathy can play a significant role in promoting mental health awareness and breaking down the stigma associated with mental illness. By approaching conversations about mental health with empathy, we can create a culture of openness and understanding. This includes:

- **Open Dialogues:** Encourage conversations about mental health in your communities, whether online or in person, to foster a culture of openness and support.

- **Educate with Empathy:** Use your understanding to educate others about the realities of mental illness, correcting misconceptions and challenging stereotypes with compassion and facts.
- **Support Inclusivity:** Advocate for inclusive policies and practices in schools, workplaces, and communities that support mental health and well-being.

Empathy, with its profound ability to connect and heal, plays a critical role in our mental health and that of those around us. By understanding and sharing the feelings of others, we not only offer support but also receive the emotional and psychological benefits of these empathetic connections. Balancing this nurturing of others with self-care ensures we can continue offering empathy without sacrificing our well-being. Promoting mental health awareness through empathetic engagement can lead to more supportive, understanding communities, shifting the narrative around mental health from one of silence and stigmatization towards one of compassion and solidarity.

Ask the Captain

How can I offer empathy to someone struggling without feeling overwhelmed myself?

Like a ship maintaining balance in turbulent waters, ensure you're anchored in self-care. Listen and support within your emotional capacity, and don't hesitate to set boundaries for your well-being. Sharing empathy is important, but so is safeguarding your own emotional deck.

Can empathy truly make a difference in someone's mental health journey?

Absolutely. Empathy can be the beacon that guides someone through their darkest nights. It offers validation, understanding, and a sense of belonging, all of which are critical buoys in the ocean of mental health recovery.

How do I navigate conversations about mental health with empathy?

Approach these conversations as you would navigate through fog—gently and with keen awareness. Listen more than you speak, validate feelings without rushing to fix them, and offer your presence as a steady light.

THE CAPTAIN'S GUIDING LIGHT

(Key Chapter Takeaways)

1. **Illuminate Understanding**: Let empathy light your understanding of others' experiences, recognizing the power of connection in healing.
2. **Anchor in Compassion**: Ground your interactions in compassion, ensuring that everyone feels seen, heard, and

valued.
3. **Navigate with Care**: Steer through conversations about mental health with sensitivity, offering support without imposing solutions.
4. **Balance with Self-Care**: Maintain your emotional equilibrium through self-care practices, ensuring you're well-equipped to offer empathy to others.
5. **Champion Open Seas**: Advocate for a culture where mental health is openly discussed and supported, contributing to a society where empathy and understanding prevail.

CHAPTER 29
BUILDING EMPATHY THROUGH VOLUNTEERING AND SOCIAL ACTION

Volunteering connects us directly to the fabric of society, weaving us into the lives of those who need our help and opening our eyes to the diverse experiences that shape human existence. Through acts of service, we step into the lives of others, not to fix them but to understand and support them. This pathway to empathy enriches our perspective, teaching us about the strength found in vulnerability and the power of collective action.

VOLUNTEERING AS A PATHWAY TO EMPATHY

Volunteering exposes us to realities outside our own, often challenging our perceptions and preconceptions. This exposure is a valuable teacher, showing us the world through others' eyes. Here's how volunteering fosters empathy:

- **Shared Experiences:** Working with those from different walks of life breaks down barriers, creating shared experiences that are fertile ground for empathy.

- **Understanding Challenges:** Whether helping at a food bank or tutoring children from underserved communities, volunteering provides insight into the challenges others face, cultivating a deeper understanding and compassion for them.
- **Personal Growth:** Witnessing resilience in the face of adversity inspires us, often leading to a profound appreciation for the strength and courage of the human spirit.

DIGITAL PLATFORMS FOR SOCIAL ACTION

In the digital age, our potential to contribute to social change extends into the online world. Digital platforms offer unique opportunities for engaging in social action, enabling us to advocate for causes we're passionate about from anywhere in the world. These platforms serve as conduits for empathy, allowing us to connect with and support communities and initiatives globally. Here are ways they facilitate social action:

- **Crowdfunding Campaigns:** Digital crowdfunding platforms amplify the impact of collective contributions by supporting projects aimed at social good, from disaster relief to funding education for underserved children.
- **Social Media Advocacy:** Using social media to raise awareness about issues can spark meaningful conversations and mobilize support. Sharing stories and information helps to educate and inspire action among our networks.
- **Virtual Volunteering:** Many organizations offer remote volunteering opportunities, from providing online tutoring to assisting with digital marketing for nonprofits. This flexibility allows individuals to lend their skills and time

to causes they care about, regardless of geographical barriers.

THE RIPPLE EFFECT OF EMPATHY

Acts of empathy and kindness, no matter how small, can set off a cascade of positive change. This ripple effect is a testament to the interconnectedness of our lives, demonstrating how individual actions can inspire and uplift communities. Consider the following:

- **Inspiring Others:** Witnessing acts of kindness and empathy often inspires onlookers to engage in their own acts of compassion, creating a chain reaction that multiplies the initial impact.
- **Building Community:** Shared acts of empathy strengthen community bonds, fostering a sense of belonging and mutual support among its members.
- **Changing Narratives:** Through empathy, we contribute to a broader cultural shift towards kindness and understanding, challenging narratives of division and highlighting our shared humanity.

CASE STUDIES OF EMPATHETIC ACTION

Real-life examples underscore the transformative power of empathy in action. Consider the following stories:

- **Community Gardens:** In a bustling city, volunteers transform vacant lots into community gardens. This initiative beautifies the neighborhood and brings residents together, fostering a sense of community and mutual support. Through gardening, participants share stories, bridging generational and cultural gaps, and cultivate a shared space of nurturing and growth.

- **Online Tutoring Program:** A college student, recognizing the challenges remote learning poses for younger students, launches a free online tutoring program. Connecting college students with K-12 students for academic support, this initiative not only aids learning but also fosters meaningful connections across different life stages. Tutors gain insight into the diverse educational challenges families face. At the same time, tutees receive personalized support, demonstrating the far-reaching impact of empathy-driven projects.
- **Virtual Support Groups:** In response to the isolation many feel during global health challenges, a nonprofit organization establishes virtual support groups. These groups offer a space for individuals to share their experiences, fears, and hopes, facilitated by trained volunteers who guide conversations with empathy and respect. Participants find solace and understanding in these shared spaces, illustrating how empathy can bridge physical distances, creating connections that support mental and emotional well-being.

Each of these examples highlights how empathy and action can foster understanding, bring people together, and drive positive change in communities. Through volunteering and social action, whether in person or digitally, we engage more deeply with the world around us, learning to view life through a lens of compassion and shared humanity. These experiences enrich our lives, broaden our perspectives, and remind us of empathy's profound impact on individuals and communities.

Ask the Captain

How do I choose where to volunteer my time to make the biggest impact?

Consider the waters you're most drawn to navigate. Reflect on causes close to your heart or issues you're passionate about. Research organizations or initiatives in those areas and consider where your unique skills and talents could be most beneficial. Like choosing a course at sea, it's about aligning your compass with the direction that feels most meaningful to you.

Can digital volunteering truly make a difference compared to being there in person?

Absolutely. In today's interconnected world, digital volunteering casts a wide net of impact. Whether it's offering your expertise, raising awareness for a cause, or supporting someone through online mentorship, your digital contribution can bridge vast distances and touch lives in far-off places. Remember, the light of your empathy shines just as brightly through a screen.

How do I balance volunteering with my personal and professional demands?

Navigating the balance between service and personal responsibilities is like steering a ship through shifting winds. Start small, perhaps with a flexible or one-time volunteering commitment, to gauge what fits best with your schedule. Remember, the journey of volunteering should be enriching, not overburdening. It's about finding a rhythm that allows you to give without draining your reserves.

THE CAPTAIN'S GUIDING LIGHT

(Key Chapter Takeaways)

1. **Set Your Compass to Empathy**: Allow empathy to guide your volunteering efforts. By understanding and connecting with the experiences of others, you enrich both their lives and your own.
2. **Chart Your Course with Intention**: Choose volunteering opportunities that resonate with your values and passions. Like selecting a charted course, this intentional choice ensures your journey is both meaningful and impactful.
3. **Harness the Power of Digital Connection**: Embrace the vast reach of digital platforms to advocate for change and offer support. The digital sea is vast and your contributions can make waves of difference across global waters.
4. **Balance the Sail with Self-Care**: Maintain an equilibrium between your altruistic endeavors and personal well-being. Volunteering should add to your life's richness, not lead to stormy seas of overwhelm you.

5. **Inspire Your Crew**: Share your experiences and the lessons learned on your volunteering journey to inspire others to embark on their own expeditions of empathy and action. Just as a lighthouse guides ships through the night, your story can illuminate the path for others to follow.

CHAPTER 30
ENCOURAGING EMPATHETIC CONVERSATIONS AT HOME

Creating a nurturing environment where every family member feels free to express their emotions and thoughts openly is akin to cultivating a garden. It requires patience, understanding, and the right conditions. In such an environment, empathy flourishes, enabling family members to connect on a deeper level, appreciate one another's feelings, and grow together as a cohesive unit.

FOSTERING AN EMPATHETIC FAMILY ENVIRONMENT

To foster a space where empathy thrives, consider these strategies:

- **Set aside Time for Family Discussions:** Regularly scheduled family meetings provide a platform for sharing feelings, concerns, and joys. It's a time when everyone can feel heard and valued.
- **Encourage Emotional Expression:** Let family members know that all emotions are valid and that expressing them is a sign of strength, not weakness. This openness paves the way for empathetic exchanges.

- **Offer Unconditional Support:** Let family members know they are supported and loved, regardless of the situation. This assurance lays the foundation for trust and open communication.

ROLE MODELING EMPATHY

As with many life skills, youth learn empathy by seeing it in action. Parents and guardians play a crucial role in this by:

- **Demonstrating Understanding and Compassion:** Show empathy in your daily interactions, not only with family members but also with friends, colleagues, and strangers. Your actions serve as a powerful example for your teens.
- **Reacting Empathetically to Mistakes:** When a child makes a mistake, address it with understanding and guidance rather than punishment. This approach teaches them that empathy is a response to experience, not judgment.

EMPATHY IN FAMILY CONFLICTS

Conflicts, while challenging, offer opportunities for practicing and reinforcing empathy. Here's how to navigate disagreements empathetically:

- **Listen Actively to All Sides:** Before jumping to conclusions, give each person involved a chance to share their perspective. This practice ensures everyone feels heard and contributes to a more nuanced understanding of the issue.

- **Acknowledge Feelings before Solving Problems:** Recognize and validate the emotions each family member is experiencing related to the conflict. Understanding each other's feelings often leads to more effective and harmonious solutions.
- **Focus on the Issue, Not the Individual:** To avoid making anyone feel attacked or defensive, keep discussions centered on the behavior or situation, not the person.

BUILDING EMPATHY THROUGH FAMILY ACTIVITIES

Shared activities can strengthen empathy among family members. Here are a few ideas:

- **Volunteer Together:** Participating in community service projects as a family can open everyone's eyes to the experiences and struggles of others, fostering a shared sense of empathy.
- **Read and Discuss Books:** Choose books that explore diverse perspectives and life experiences. Discussing the characters' feelings and decisions can deepen family members' understanding of different viewpoints.
- **Play Role-Reversal Games:** Games where family members "walk in each other's shoes" by acting out each other's roles can be a fun and enlightening way to understand different perspectives within the family.

In essence, empathy within the family acts as the glue that binds members together, creating a supportive and understanding environment where everyone can thrive. Families can strengthen their connections and navigate life's challenges more harmoniously by fostering open communication, modeling empathetic behavior, addressing conflicts with understanding, and engaging in activities that build empathy.

As we close this chapter, it's clear that empathy is more than a soft skill—it's a foundational element that enriches our lives, transforming our relationships and interactions. From the comfort of our homes to the vast digital world, practicing empathy can change perspectives, bridge gaps, and cultivate a culture of understanding and kindness. As we move forward, let's carry these insights into our communities and beyond, continuing to explore the profound impact empathy can have on our collective well-being.

Ask the Captain

How can I encourage my family to be more open about their feelings?

Like inviting sunlight into a garden, create a warm and inviting atmosphere where sharing is encouraged and valued. Lead by example, sharing your own feelings openly and responding to theirs with genuine interest and care.

What if a family member is resistant to participating in empathetic practices?

Like a plant that's slow to bloom, give them time and space. Continue to nurture an empathetic environment and demonstrate understanding. Sometimes, observing the positive impact on others can gradually encourage participation.

How do I handle a situation where empathy leads to intense emotional discussions?

When the sea is stormy, it's essential to anchor in calmness and patience. Acknowledge and validate the emotions present, and guide the conversation gently, ensuring everyone feels heard and supported.

THE CAPTAIN'S GUIDING LIGHT

(Key Chapter Takeaways)

1. **Cultivate a Space for Growth**: Create an environment where every family member feels safe and encouraged to express their emotions, much like a well-tended garden.
2. **Lead by Example**: Demonstrate empathy in your interactions, showing your family the beauty and strength that comes from understanding and compassion.
3. **Tend to Each Plant**: Recognize and respect the individual emotional needs and expressions of each family member, fostering a rich diversity of understanding.
4. **Embrace the Weeds**: Approach conflicts with empathy, using them as opportunities to strengthen family bonds and deepen mutual understanding.

5. **Harvest Together**: Engage in activities that build empathy as a family, enriching your collective emotional landscape and drawing you closer to one another.

PART FOUR
SOLVING DISPUTES CONSTRUCTIVELY

Picture this: Two friends, both avid fans of the same basketball team, find themselves in a heated argument over which player is the most valuable. The discussion, which started as a fun debate, quickly escalates into a shouting match, leaving both parties frustrated and the friendship strained. It's a scenario that's all too familiar, whether the argument is about sports, politics, or which movie to watch. Here, the challenge isn't just about resolving the dispute but understanding why it happened in the first place.

In this chapter, we delve into the roots of conflicts, especially among teens, and explore how identifying these origins paves the way for effective resolution. By understanding where disagreements stem from and recognizing our role in them, we can approach conflicts with a mindset geared towards finding solutions rather than winning arguments.

CHAPTER 31
IDENTIFYING THE ROOT CAUSES OF CONFLICTS

Diving into the heart of disagreements reveals that teen conflicts are not just surface skirmishes but are deeply rooted in underlying issues. Identifying these roots can illuminate the path to resolution and understanding, transforming conflicts from barriers into bridges of growth and connection.

Understanding Conflict Origins

Like explorers of the ocean's mysterious depths, we can uncover the hidden undercurrents that drive conflicts. This understanding empowers us, transforming the foggy waters of disagreement into clearer currents of resolution and growth:

- **Misunderstandings**: Conflict often ignites from miscommunication, such as when we don't express ourselves clearly or don't understand others correctly, or misconceptions, which are mistaken beliefs. This highlights the importance of clarity and open dialogue.

- **Jealousy and Competition**: The turbulent seas of envy and rivalry can disrupt the calmest waters, stemming from comparisons in achievements or social dynamics.
- **Differing Values and Beliefs**: As teens chart their courses, diverging values and beliefs can clash, leading to passionate debates and sometimes conflicts.

SELF-REFLECTION IN CONFLICT

By turning the compass inward and reflecting on our role in a conflict, we can reveal insights previously obscured by the storm of emotions. This introspection, though challenging, is a crucial and mature step in navigating toward resolution and personal growth.

THE ROLE OF COMMUNICATION IN NAVIGATING CONFLICTS

Our communication methods hold the power to calm the winds of conflict or exacerbate them. By choosing words and tones that reflect understanding and respect, we can steer conversations toward peaceful shores. This realization empowers us to make a positive change. Conversely, harsh language may push us further into the storm.

NAVIGATING THROUGH CONFLICTS TOWARDS GROWTH

Understanding the roots of our conflicts and embracing a mindset aimed at resolution rather than conquest can transform our interactions. Whereas conquest is about winning at all costs, resolution is about finding a solution that benefits everyone involved. It strengthens our relationships, nurtures personal development, and enriches our journey through the teenage years. By approaching disagreements with openness, empathy, and a willingness to understand, we resolve the immediate issues and build a foundation of resilience and mutual respect that will guide us through all of life's conflicts.

Ask the Captain

How can I prevent small misunderstandings from turning into big conflicts?

Just like correcting a small course error early can prevent a ship from veering off track, addressing misunderstandings promptly and openly can prevent them from escalating. Aim for clear communication and don't hesitate to seek clarification if you sense confusion.

What if I realize I'm the one who escalated the conflict?

Recognizing your role in a conflict is like finding your bearings after being lost at sea. It's never too late to adjust your course. Apologize sincerely and discuss ways to move forward, showing that you're committed to better navigation in the future.

How do I handle a conflict when the other person refuses to communicate?

Sometimes, despite our best efforts, the other person may not be ready to engage. Give them space, like allowing the sea time to calm after a storm, and let them know you're open to talking when they're ready. Patience and understanding can sometimes reopen closed channels of communication.

THE CAPTAIN'S GUIDING LIGHT

(Key Chapter Takeaways)

1. **Seek Understanding, Not Victory**: Approach conflicts with the goal of understanding the other person's perspective rather than winning the argument. This mindset can lead to more productive and empathetic resolutions.
2. **Embrace Open Dialogue**: Keeping the lines of communication open, even in rough waters, ensures that misunderstandings are cleared up quickly, preventing them from evolving into larger conflicts.
3. **Reflect before You React**: Take a moment to consider your response in a conflict. Like when a captain assesses the best course of action before giving an order, thoughtful responses can lead to more peaceful outcomes.
4. **Learn from Every Storm**: Each conflict offers lessons on communication, empathy, and self-awareness. Reflect on these experiences to improve how you navigate future disagreements.
5. **Cultivate a Climate of Empathy**: Foster an environment, whether at home or among friends, where everyone feels

safe to express their thoughts and feelings. This supportive atmosphere can significantly reduce the frequency and intensity of conflicts.

CHAPTER 32
COMMUNICATION STRATEGIES FOR CONFLICT RESOLUTION

Conflicts are inevitable in the vast sea of human connection, like sudden squalls that can either test or strengthen the bonds of our relationships. The mastery of effective communication serves as our compass and anchor, guiding us through these storms with grace and mutual respect. This chapter delves into the art of communication strategies that foster understanding and resolution, ensuring that even the most turbulent waters can lead to peaceful harbors.

TRANSPARENT AND HONEST EXPRESSION: THE BEACON OF UNDERSTANDING

Clear and honest communication shines as a beacon through the fog of conflict, guiding both parties toward mutual understanding.

- **Speak Your Truth Calmly**: Like a lighthouse provides guidance, expressing your thoughts and feelings calmly ensures your message is seen and heard.

- **Avoid Assumptions**: Assumptions are the hidden reefs that can sink ships of dialogue. Approach each conversation with an open mind, ready to navigate through the words of the other with curiosity and openness.
- **Transparency Is Key**: Just as clear waters allow for safe passage, transparency in your words fosters trust and clarity, which is crucial for navigating toward resolution.

ACTIVE LISTENING FOR UNDERSTANDING: THE ART OF RECEIVING

Active listening involves not just hearing but also receiving—taking in the entire message, emotions, and meanings conveyed by the other.

- **Fully Engage**: To truly listen is to offer your undivided attention, turning off distractions and focusing solely on the speaker, as a ship focuses on its guiding star.
- **Mirror Emotions**: Reflecting back the emotions you hear can validate the speaker's feelings, showing you are genuinely alongside them on this journey.
- **Clarify and Affirm**: Asking questions for clarity and affirming what you've understood ensures no message is lost in the storm, much like confirming coordinates while navigating treacherous waters.

THE POWER OF 'I' STATEMENTS: STEERING AWAY FROM BLAME

'I' statements are the rudder that steers conversations away from the rocks of blame and towards the calm waters of personal experience and responsibility.

- **Structure Your Sentences**: Begin with "I feel," "I need," or "I think" to focus on your perspective, which help you chart your own course through the sea of conflict.
- **Express, Don't Accuse**: This approach transforms potential accusations into expressions of personal feeling, like changing rough winds into guiding breezes.
- **Personal Accountability**: Taking ownership of your feelings and actions fosters a more mature and respectful dialogue, like a captain taking responsibility for their ship.

TIMING AND SETTING: CHOOSING THE RIGHT MOMENT AND PLACE

The timing and setting of a conversation can influence its direction as much as the winds and tides can affect a voyage.

- **Choose a Calm Moment**: Wait for the emotional storms to pass before initiating discussions, ensuring both parties can navigate with clear heads and calm hearts.
- **Privacy Matters**: Discussing sensitive issues away from the crowds creates a safe harbor for open and vulnerable communication.
- **Neutral Ground**: A neutral setting can level the playing field, making it easier to find common ground, much like two ships meeting peacefully in open waters.

By integrating these strategies into our interactions, especially during conflicts, we chart a course through disagreements and cultivate more profound, more meaningful connections. These practices ensure that no matter how challenging, every conflict becomes an opportunity for growth, understanding, and stronger bonds. Let us remember that it's not the presence of storms that defines our journey but how we choose to navigate them.

Ask the Captain

How can I keep calm and not get defensive when I'm misunderstood?

Picture yourself as the captain in the eye of a storm—steadiness is key. Take a deep breath and remind yourself that the goal is understanding, not winning. Reflect on your feelings using 'I' statements to express yourself without escalating the situation. Remember, every skilled captain was once a learner; practice patience with yourself and others.

What if the other person isn't willing to communicate effectively?

Sometimes, you may find yourself navigating choppy waters where the other party isn't ready to sail in the same direction. In such cases, maintain your course of respectful and clear communication. Offer them space and time, like waiting for the sea to calm, and suggest revisiting the conversation later. Your steadiness may encourage them to open up in time.

How do I approach a conversation I know will be difficult?

Prepare as a captain does before setting sail into the unknown. Reflect on what you want to communicate and consider the best setting and timing for the discussion. Approach the conversation with an open heart and mind, ready to navigate through rough waters with empathy and understanding. And remember, the goal is to reach a peaceful shore together, not to journey alone.

THE CAPTAIN'S GUIDING LIGHT

(Key Chapter Takeaways)

1. **Chart Your Course with Clarity and Honesty**: Like a ship guided by the stars, let your communication be guided by the light of truth and transparency. Speak your truth calmly and clearly, ensuring your words reflect your genuine thoughts and feelings.
2. **Anchor in Active Listening**: The calmest ports are found by listening to the sea; similarly, the deepest understanding comes from actively listening to others. Engage fully, reflect emotions, and clarify messages to ensure no word is lost in the wind.
3. **Steer with 'I' Statements**: Navigate away from the rocky shores of blame. Use 'I' statements to express your feelings and needs, keeping the waters between you and the other person calm and navigable.
4. **Select the Right Tide and Time**: Timing and setting are the currents that can carry a conversation to peaceful or stormy ends. Choose a moment of calm and a private, neutral setting to ensure a safe journey through the conversation.

5. **Be the Compassionate Captain**: Above all, lead with empathy and understanding. Remember that every conflict is an opportunity to deepen connections and learn more about navigating the complex seas of human relationships.

CHAPTER 33
THE ROLE OF COMPROMISE IN SOLVING DISAGREEMENTS

In the dynamic realm of relationships, the art of compromise shines as a crucial skill, guiding us through potential conflicts to the shores of resolution and mutual respect. It's not about giving in but steering our way towards a solution that all parties can support, ensuring the strength and stability of our connections.

DEFINING COMPROMISE: THE CHART FOR MUTUAL UNDERSTANDING

Compromise is the compass that directs us towards balanced solutions, where each party is heard and satisfied. However, they may only receive some of the satisfaction they initially sought and instead find new satisfaction in a mutually beneficial resolution.

- **Mutual Concession**: It's akin to plotting a course where both captains adjust their routes to avoid collision and ensure safe passage.
- **Collaborative Effort**: Like a crew working together to navigate narrow straits, compromise requires teamwork and communication. This cooperative nature empowers

each individual to contribute to the solution, fostering a sense of involvement and shared responsibility.
- **Balanced Outcomes**: The aim is to dock at a port where all can disembark, feel respected and valued, and have their most crucial cargo intact.

FINDING COMMON GROUND: THE MAP TO SHARED TERRITORIES

Discovering common ground is akin to finding hidden treasures in the vast ocean of interaction. It's on these shared sands that the foundation for compromise is built.

- **Shared Goals and Values**: Identifying these is like charting stars that guide both parties, providing a fixed point of reference amidst negotiation storms.
- **Active Exploration**: This journey of discovery requires open dialogue and a willingness to dive into the depths of the disagreement, unearthing areas of agreement that might not be immediately visible.

STEPS TO A FAIR COMPROMISE: NAVIGATING THE NEGOTIATION SEAS

The journey to compromise involves distinct navigational steps, each requiring attention and care to ensure a fair and equitable resolution.

- **Open Dialogue**: Like sending out scouts to map the terrain, this step involves laying out the landscape of the disagreement, ensuring all perspectives are heard and acknowledged.

- **Identify Non-negotiables**: Marking the reefs and shoals on a map and understanding each party's non-negotiables ensures safe navigation, avoiding areas of potential shipwreck.
- **Brainstorm Solutions**: This creative brainstorming is like charting potential courses, considering winds, currents, and obstacles to find the most viable route.
- **Agree on a Plan**: Choosing the best course and committing to it is akin to setting sail with all hands on deck, dedicated to the journey ahead.

WHEN COMPROMISE ISN'T POSSIBLE: CHARTING A DIFFERENT COURSE

Sometimes, the seas are too rough and a direct path to compromise can't be found. In these cases, agreeing to disagree becomes a necessary detour.

- **Respecting Differences**: Recognizing the vastness of the sea and the variety of paths it holds, we understand that not all journeys will converge.
- **Maintaining Connection**: The anchor of our relationships, even amidst disagreement, ensures that the bonds remain solid for future dialogue.

Compromise, in the realm of relationships, is an art form as nuanced and vital as the skills of an experienced navigator. It requires patience, understanding, and a commitment to mutual respect. By engaging in this process, we resolve the immediate disputes and strengthen our bonds, enriching the tapestry of our connections with threads of empathy, flexibility, and enduring respect. As we navigate the waters of compromise, we learn that the actual destination is not just resolution but also a deeper understanding and appreciation of those with whom we share our journey.

Ask the Captain

How do I initiate a conversation about compromise without seeming like I'm giving up on my values?

Begin by affirming your commitment to finding a solution that respects everyone's core values, including your own. Clarify that compromise isn't about abandoning one's beliefs but about navigating together towards a solution that all parties can accept. It's like charting a course that avoids the storm while still reaching the destination.

What if we can't find any common ground?

Sometimes, the seas seem too vast to find a meeting point in. In such cases, consider bringing in a neutral third party, like a mediator, who can help identify unseen commonalities or suggest new paths to agreement. It's akin to having an experienced navigator join you to point out navigable waters you might have missed.

How do I deal with feeling like I've compromised too much?

Reflect on the compromises made and assess whether your core needs and values are still intact. Compromise should feel like a balanced exchange, not a loss. If you're feeling depleted, it might be time to renegotiate, ensuring that future agreements more evenly distribute the give-and-take. Remember, even the sturdiest ships need maintenance to stay afloat.

THE CAPTAIN'S GUIDING LIGHT

(Key Chapter Takeaways)

1. **Mutual Concession as Cooperation**: View each concession not as losing a piece of your cargo but as trading it for something equally valuable to ensure a smoother journey for all involved.
2. **Shared Goals, Shared Compass**: Keep the shared goals as your compass point, guiding discussions and decisions. It's the lighthouse that keeps you oriented amidst the fog of disagreement.
3. **Active Exploration for Common Ground**: Venture into discussions with the spirit of an explorer. Seek out the uncharted territories of common interests and values that lie beneath the surface of apparent discord.
4. **Navigate with Open Dialogue**: Clear, open communication is your map through the seas of conflict. Chart your course with honesty and listen intently to the currents of conversation to avoid hidden reefs.
5. **Embrace Flexibility in Your Course**: Be willing to adjust your sails. A flexible approach allows you to navigate

through storms of contention to the calm waters of agreement, even if it means taking a route you hadn't initially planned.

CHAPTER 34
COOL WATERS: CHILLING OUT WHEN CONVERSATIONS HEAT UP

Ever felt like you're surfing on a massive wave during an argument that's about to crash big time? That's when things get too heated, and it's important to know how to steer back to the chill zone. Here's your guide to not wiping out when the convo gets stormy.

SPOTTING THE WAVE BEFORE IT BREAKS

First, you have to recognize when things are starting to get rough. Maybe voices are getting louder, or someone's throwing around "always" and "never" like they're handing out flyers. Body language can shout louder than words, too—arms crossed, eyes rolling, or that intense stare-down. These are your signs to change course.

RIDING THE CHILL CURRENT

When the seas of chat start to get stormy, you've got some slick moves to keep your surfboard steady:

- **Deep Dives for Breath**: Yep, the good old deep breaths. They're like diving under a wave—they help you keep cool and prevent you from getting dragged down by the current.
- **Pause the Paddle**: Hold up before you snap back with a comeback. Counting to ten in your head allows you to pick your next move wisely.
- **Time-Out on the Beach**: If things are getting too gnarly, suggest taking a break from the talk. A bit of time chilling on the sand can do wonders.

WHY IT'S WORTH STEERING CLEAR OF THE STORM

Dialing down the heat isn't about bailing on the wave; it's about making sure everyone gets to keep surfing together. It keeps the vibes good and ensures no one ends up with a nasty wipeout that hurts long-term feelings.

HOW TO KEEP THE WATERS CALM

So, you've spotted a big one rolling in — here's how to keep riding smoothly:

- **Speak Easy**: Use words that cool things down, like "I get where you're coming from" or "Let's figure this out together." It's like tossing a lifeline to someone struggling in the water.

- **Feel Their Flow**: Letting them know you see they're upset, like "I see you're really into this," shows you're not there to argue but to understand. It's like acknowledging the wave they're riding.
- **Find a New Wave**: Sometimes, shifting the chat to something chill for a second can break the tension. "Hey, before we dive back in, did you catch the game last night?"
- **Plan to Paddle Out Again**: If the waves are too wild, it's cool to say, "Let's talk about this later when things aren't so heated." It means you're open to catching up once the storm passes.

Mastering chilling out heated convos is like learning to surf big waves. It takes practice, patience, and knowing when to ride and when to chill. By keeping your head cool and your words kind, you'll dodge wipeouts and help everyone enjoy the surf together. And who knows? You might find some epic waves of understanding along the way.

Ask the Captain

How can I calm the situation when the other person keeps escalating?

Imagine you're steering through rough seas; the key is to maintain your course calmly. Continue using calming language and acknowledging their feelings, showing you're a safe harbor, not the storm. If needed, suggest a temporary retreat to calmer waters—a pause in the conversation—to allow emotions to settle.

What if my attempts at de-escalation are met with more anger?

Sometimes, despite your best efforts, the winds will howl louder. If your attempts to calm the waters seem to stir the storm, it might be time to dock the ship for a while—take a more substantial break from the discussion. It's okay to say, "I think we need a little time to cool off. Let's revisit this later when we can talk more calmly."

Is walking away from a heated situation seen as giving up?

Not at all. Think of it as charting a course for clearer skies. Walking away can be a strategic decision to prevent damage to the ship and crew—your well-being and relationship. It's a sign of wisdom to recognize when a storm can't be navigated in the moment and choose instead to wait for a better time to sail back into the discussion.

THE CAPTAIN'S GUIDING LIGHT

(Key Chapter Takeaways)

1. **Recognize the Storm Clouds**: Pay attention to the early signs of emotional escalation—raised voices, absolute statements, defensive body language—and prepare to adjust your sails.

2. **Steady Your Ship with Emotional Regulation**: Use deep breathing, pauses, and timeouts to keep your emotions in check, ensuring you can navigate through rough waters without capsizing.
3. **Use Calming Signals**: Phrases that acknowledge the other person's feelings and intentions to find common ground act as buoys, guiding the conversation back to safety.
4. **Acknowledge and Validate**: Sometimes, simply recognizing the other person's emotional state can reduce the swell, making it easier to navigate back to calmer dialogue.
5. **Know When to Seek Harbor**: Recognizing when to take a break from the conversation can prevent the storm from causing lasting damage, allowing both parties to return to the discussion with clearer heads and calmer hearts.

CHAPTER 35
APOLOGIZING AND FORGIVING: STEPS TOWARD HEALING

In the intricate dance of human interaction, missteps are inevitable. However, the steps we take next—apologizing and forgiving—can either lead us back into harmony or further apart. This section delves into the profound significance of a genuine apology and the transformative power of forgiveness. These are not just steps, but essential elements in the journey of rebuilding trust and healing after a misstep.

THE POWER OF A GENUINE APOLOGY

A heartfelt apology transcends the mere acknowledgment of wrongdoing; it's a vulnerable act of taking responsibility and expressing a genuine desire to mend what's been broken. This is not just about the other person; it's about you, too. A genuine apology can bring a sense of emotional relief, knowing that you've done your part to make amends. Here are the elements that make an apology sincere:

- **Acknowledgment of the Hurt Caused:** Clearly stating what you did wrong shows that you understand the impact of your actions.
- **Expressing Remorse:** Conveying genuine remorse demonstrates that you regret not just the consequences but the hurt your actions caused.
- **Commitment to Change:** A vital component of a genuine apology is a promise to avoid repeating the behavior, showing that you're invested in change and growth.
- Making Amends: Whenever possible, offer to make things right. This might mean replacing something you broke or rectifying a mistake.

ACCEPTING APOLOGIES

Receiving an apology with an open heart is not just a passive act; it's a powerful choice. It involves acknowledging your own feelings and deciding how to respond. Here's how to accept apologies in a way that fosters healing and reconciliation:

- **Listen Fully:** Before responding, listen to the entire apology without interrupting. This allows you to fully understand the intent and depth of the other person's remorse.
- **Express Your Feelings:** Share how the incident affected you, but try to do so without casting blame. This can be therapeutic and can help the other person understand your perspective.
- **Decide to Forgive:** Forgiveness is a choice. While it's often a difficult one, it's an essential step towards healing. It doesn't mean forgetting or excusing the behavior but rather letting go of resentment.

- **Communicate Your Acceptance:** Clearly stating that you accept the apology can provide closure to both parties and open the door to rebuilding trust.

THE PROCESS OF FORGIVENESS

Forgiveness is not just an act of kindness towards another; it's a transformative journey of personal growth. It's the process of releasing anger and resentment and stepping into a brighter, more peaceful future. Here are the benefits and steps involved in forgiving:

- **Emotional Freedom:** Holding onto anger ties you to the past. Forgiveness allows you to move forward with peace.
- **Health Benefits:** Letting go of grudges can positively affect your mental and physical health, reducing stress and promoting well-being.
- **Understanding:** Try to see the situation from the other person's perspective. This doesn't justify their actions but can help you understand them better.
- **Letting Go:** Forgiveness involves actively choosing to release feelings of resentment. It's a personal journey that takes time and, often, repeated effort.

REBUILDING TRUST

Trust, once broken, is not easily repaired. It requires time, effort, and a commitment to change. Here are strategies to gradually restore trust after a conflict or misunderstanding, a crucial step in the journey of relationship repair:

- **Consistency:** Show through your actions that you've changed. Consistent behavior over time is critical to rebuilding trust.
- **Transparency:** Be open about your thoughts and feelings. This openness can prevent misunderstandings and demonstrate your commitment to honesty.
- **Patience:** Understand that regaining trust doesn't happen overnight. Be patient with the process and with each other.
- **Reaffirm Commitment:** Regularly reaffirm your commitment to both the relationship and maintaining the changes you promised.

In navigating the complexities of human relationships, apologies and forgiveness serve as vital tools for healing and growth. We take responsibility for our actions through genuine apologies and express our desire to mend what's been damaged. By choosing to forgive, we free ourselves from the weight of past hurts and open up the possibility of rebuilding trust and restoring harmony. This journey of making amends and granting forgiveness is a testament to the resilience and depth of our connections, a dance of give-and-take that can lead us back into step with one another when navigated with care and sincerity.

Ask the Captain

What if I apologize and they don't forgive me?

Imagine you've carefully patched up a sail after a storm. You've done your part, but the wind's reaction isn't up to you. Offer your apology sincerely, like mending that sail with care, but know that their process of forgiveness might take more time. Sometimes, the seas calm down slower than we wish. Keep showing through your actions that you're genuine in your regret and commitment to do better.

How can I forgive someone when I still feel hurt?

Forgiveness is like steering your ship through foggy waters; you might not see clearly at first. It's okay to feel hurt; forgiveness doesn't mean those feelings vanish instantly. Begin by acknowledging your pain and giving yourself permission to feel it. Then, when you're ready, slowly lift the anchor of resentment. This doesn't mean you forget what happened, but you can choose to sail beyond it for your own peace.

How do I rebuild trust after it's been broken?

Rebuilding trust is like repairing a beloved but weather-beaten ship — it takes time, effort, and patience. Start with small steps and consistent actions that show you're true to your word. Be as open as you can about your thoughts and feelings, like sharing your navigation map. It's a journey, and every act of sincerity is a plank in the rebuild of your ship of trust.

THE CAPTAIN'S GUIDING LIGHT

(Key Chapter Takeaways)

1. **Acknowledge the Damage**: Recognize and clearly state the hurt caused. It's like admitting a navigational error — it's the first step to setting things right.
2. **Show Genuine Remorse**: Let your sincerity shine like a lighthouse, guiding the way back to trust. Your genuine regret can illuminate the path to forgiveness.
3. **Commit to Change**: Promise to steer a better course and show through consistent actions that you're dedicated to keeping the ship on a new, respectful heading.
4. **Make Amends**: Where possible, do what you can to repair the damage. It might not fix everything, but it's a crucial part of mending the sails.
5. **Choose to Forgive**: Forgiveness requires setting sail from a harbor of hurt, allowing you to explore new horizons. It's for your peace and progress, freeing you from the anchor of resentment.

CHAPTER 36
CHARTING A COURSE THROUGH TEEN CONFLICTS: THE ART OF MEDIATION

Sailing the sometimes stormy seas of teenage conflicts might seem like you're navigating by starlight, hoping to find peace on distant shores. Yet, in these swirling waters, a method known as mediation acts like a lighthouse, guiding ships to resolution without crashing on the rocks of confrontation. This chapter illuminates how mediation, with its focus on collaboration and understanding, offers teens a map to traverse disputes with their crewmates gracefully.

DISCOVERING MEDIATION

Mediation is a calm port in the storm. It provides a structured yet adaptable approach in which an impartial navigator or mediator aids those adrift in disagreement. This navigator helps them anchor in a resolution they all accept. This method steers clear of the win-lose mindset of arguments and encourages teens to work together and chart a course to mutual understanding.

THE MEDIATOR'S COMPASS

Like a skilled captain, the mediator directs the conversation's course, ensuring that the journey is fair and focused. Essential traits of a mediator include:

- **Neutrality**: Keeping the compass steady, the mediator remains unbiased, ensuring all voices are heard equally.
- **Communication Skills**: The mediator has a knack for clear signaling, which helps clarify misunderstandings and expresses solutions in a way that all crew members understand.
- **Empathy**: By recognizing and acknowledging each person's perspective without judgment, the mediator fosters a sense of trust and openness.
- **Problem-Solving Prowess**: By identifying the dispute's true undercurrents, the mediator assists in navigating towards creative and peaceful solutions.

THE VOYAGE OF MEDIATION

Embarking on mediation follows several vital steps in order to chart a course from discord to harmony:

- **Preparation**: The mediator meets with each party individually before the session to map out their perspectives and establish trust.
- **Establishing Rules of Engagement**: The session begins with setting basic protocols, such as speaking in turn, maintaining respect, and keeping discussions confidential.
- **Sharing the Helm**: Each person gets a turn to share their story uninterrupted, laying the foundation for mutual

understanding.
- **Identifying the Navigational Hazards**: The mediator helps pinpoint the core issues, separating them from emotional whirlpools and side currents.
- **Exploring Uncharted Waters**: They brainstorm possible solutions together, with the mediator ensuring every suggestion is explored.
- **Reaching Safe Harbor**: An agreement that meets everyone's needs and resolves the conflict is sought through dialogue and negotiation.

GATHERING THE CREW: TRAINING AND RESOURCES

For teens interested in becoming peer mediators, numerous resources and training opportunities are available to equip them with the skills needed to confidently steer their ships. These include:

- **Workshops and Training**: Schools and community organizations often offer programs teaching the essentials of mediation and strategies for peaceful conflict resolution.
- **Online Navigation Courses**: Various digital platforms provide courses in mediation, allowing teens to learn at their own pace, guided by the stars.
- **Mentorship Programs**: Learning from seasoned mediators can provide invaluable insights and guidance for navigating real-world conflicts.
- **Practice Voyages**: Engaging in role-playing exercises and simulations allows teens to apply their skills in a supportive setting and learn to navigate conflicts with aplomb.

By embracing mediation, teens can transform how they face disputes, turning potential clashes into opportunities for connection and growth. This journey fosters empathy and cooperation among peers. It equips teens with navigational skills to guide them through life's tumultuous waters, ensuring they can always find their way to peaceful shores.

Ask the Captain

How do I start mediating a conflict between friends?

Begin by inviting them to a neutral space where everyone feels comfortable. Express your intention to help find a fair resolution, not to take sides. Set some ground rules, like allowing each person to speak without interruption and approaching the discussion with an open mind.

What if the other parties don't want to participate in mediation?

You can't force someone to mediate if they're not ready. Give them some space and time. Share how mediation might benefit everyone involved, but also respect their decision. Sometimes, just knowing the option is available can be a comfort.

How can I stay neutral when I have my own opinion about the conflict?

Staying neutral is challenging, especially if you're close to the situation. Remind yourself that your role is to facilitate understanding, not to judge. Focus on listening and helping the parties communicate their feelings and needs more clearly. If you find it too difficult to remain unbiased, it might be helpful to suggest someone else to mediate.

THE CAPTAIN'S GUIDING LIGHT

(Key Chapter Takeaways)

1. **Understanding the Map**: Remember, successful mediation requires understanding both sides. Your role is like a navigator's, helping to chart a course through troubled waters to a place of mutual understanding.
2. **Neutral Waters**: Stay in the middle ground, maintaining neutrality to ensure all parties feel heard and respected. Think of yourself as the calm eye of the storm, where peace reigns despite the chaos.
3. **Open Channels**: Promote open and respectful communication. Encourage everyone to express their thoughts and feelings without fear of judgment, as if they're in open seas where all ships can sail freely.
4. **Navigating through Empathy**: Use empathy to understand each perspective. It's the compass that guides you to deeper understanding, allowing you to navigate even the most treacherous waters.
5. **Harbor of Resolution**: Aim for a solution that respects everyone's needs and concerns. Like guiding ships into

harbor, ensure everyone arrives safely at a place of agreement and understanding.

CHAPTER 37
RESOLVING CONFLICTS WITHOUT ADULT INTERVENTION

Navigating the turbulent seas of adolescence often means encountering storms of conflict among peers. Yet, there's a certain sense of adventure and growth in learning to chart these waters independently without always calling for the lifeline of adult intervention. This journey, though challenging, tests our mettle and arms young navigators with the compass of responsibility and the map of interpersonal skills crucial for the voyage into adulthood.

EMPOWERING SELF-RESOLUTION

The ability of teens to captain their own ships through the choppy waters of disagreement is a testament to their growing wisdom and self-reliance. This autonomy, when encouraged, signals a deep trust in their capabilities to find safe passage to resolution, fostering essential skills for navigating life's broader oceans.

SKILLS FOR INDEPENDENT CONFLICT RESOLUTION

Mastering the helm of conflict resolution requires a keen set of skills, each acting as a crucial navigational instrument:

- **Effective Communication**: Like a well-manned lighthouse, it ensures clear signals are sent and received, preventing unnecessary collisions through active listening, understanding hidden currents of non-verbal cues, and articulating thoughts with respect.
- **Empathy**: Viewing the horizon from another's deck is a powerful tool in conflict resolution. It promotes understanding and connection, often revealing the true nature of the conflict and charting a course toward familiar shores. Remember, empathy is not just a skill; it's a compass that can guide you to a peaceful resolution.
- **Problem-Solving**: Treating conflicts as uncharted territories to be explored for mutual benefit rather than battlegrounds encourages creative mapping of solutions where compromise may be the treasure.
- **Emotional Intelligence**: Using EI to steady one's vessel amidst emotional squalls and recognize when others are adrift can prevent escalation and guide all parties to calmer waters.

WHEN TO SIGNAL FOR HELP

There are storms too fierce for young sailors to face alone. Recognizing when to send up a flare for adult guidance, such as in situations involving bullying, threats, or harm, is not an admission of defeat but a wise call to ensure safe navigation. It's a sign of strength and a reminder that support is always available.

CREATING A CULTURE OF PEER SUPPORT

Building a crew of support among peers can transform the choppy seas of conflict into opportunities for camaraderie and growth:

- **Respect**: A code of conduct where every voice is valued steadies the ship, fostering dialogue over discord.
- **Openness**: Encouraging a crew to be open to diverse viewpoints ensures smooth sailing through potential misunderstandings.
- **Confidentiality**: Trust is the anchor of peer resolution; maintaining the privacy of discussions ensures a secure deck for open exchanges.
- **Skill Sharing**: Passing on the art of navigating through conflict is not just a way to resolve the current issue but also strengthens the fleet. It prepares all for future voyages of disagreement, ensuring that the crew is always ready to face any storm that comes their way.

In mastering the art of resolving conflicts without constant reliance on adult intervention, teens not only chart their course through immediate challenges but also prepare for the vast seas of adult life. It's a journey that builds confidence, empathy, and a profound understanding of the power of peaceful resolution.

Ask the Captain

What's the first step in navigating a conflict on my own?

Begin by anchoring yourself in calmness. Approach the other party with the intention to understand and resolve, setting a course for open and respectful communication.

How do I keep my cool when the waves of emotion run high?

Take a moment to steady your ship. Deep breaths and a pause can be your compass, helping you navigate through emotional turbulence with a clear head.

What if we can't find a resolution and the storm continues to rage?

Sometimes, the waters are too rough to navigate alone. In those cases, it's wise to send a signal for help, bringing in a neutral adult to mediate the squall, ensuring everyone reaches safe harbor.

THE CAPTAIN'S GUIDING LIGHT

(Key Chapter Takeaways)

1. **Chart Your Course**: Remember, the goal of resolving conflicts is to find a solution that all crew members can navigate by, not to win the battle.
2. **Steady as She Goes**: Maintain an even keel by keeping communication open and respectful, even when the seas are rough.
3. **All Hands on Deck**: Engage everyone involved in finding the resolution. A crew that works together stays together, even through the toughest storms.
4. **Navigate with Compassion**: Empathy is your compass in understanding the emotions and perspectives of your fellow sailors, guiding you to peaceful shores.
5. **Safe Harbor**: Reaching a resolution is like finding safe harbor after a storm. It's a journey that requires patience, skill, and sometimes, the courage to ask for help.

CHAPTER 38
NAVIGATING THROUGH STORMY SEAS: LESSONS FROM THE HELM

Embarking on the journey of adolescence, we often sail into the uncharted waters of conflicts, where storms rage and the waves of disagreement threaten to capsize our ships. Yet, within these turbulent waters, we discover invaluable treasures: lessons of understanding, growth, and resilience. Each resolved conflict, much like navigating through a storm, teaches us how to mend our sails and steer more wisely in the future.

GROWTH OPPORTUNITIES FROM CHARTED CONFLICTS

After weathering a storm of disagreement, the calm seas that follow often hold reflections of our voyage – insights into the hearts and minds of our crew (our peers) and a deeper understanding of our own navigational errors and strengths. These encounters with conflict, when approached with a captain's resolve to find peaceful shores, illuminate paths to:

- **A Broad Horizon of Empathy:** We can learn to understand the currents that drive others' actions and feelings.
- **Greater Self-Awareness:** Introspection reveals the contours of our own emotional landscapes.
- Strengthened Bonds with our Crew: Braving the storm together fortifies trust and camaraderie.

REFLECTIVE PRACTICES IN CALMER WATERS

Taking the helm for some self-reflection guides us toward personal enlightenment and preparation for future voyages in the tranquility that follows the storm. Engage in practices such as:

- **Journaling:** Charting our journey through journaling helps capture the essence of the storm, our navigation tactics, and the path to resolution.
- **Self-Assessment:** Plotting our emotional and behavioral course through the conflict can uncover areas ripe for growth.
- **Collect Feedback:** Seeking the perspective of our crew enriches our understanding of the voyage's impact and our role as a navigator.

SHARING THE CHARTED COURSE

Sharing the map of our journey through conflict with fellow navigators lights the way for others navigating through their storms. This sharing:

- **Lights the Way for Others:** We can offer a lighthouse of support and guidance for those adrift in similar seas.

- **Educates:** When we circulate the charts of effective navigation strategies, we enrich the collective knowledge on steering through conflicts.
- **Builds Community Support:** When we share our experiences, we weave a more substantial net of communal support, underscoring the universality of conflict and the shared victory in resolution.

Preventive Measures for Smoother Sailing

With a captain's eye, we learn that certain practices and communication strategies act as lighthouses, warning us of potential storms ahead and guiding us toward smoother sailing. These preventive measures:

- **Emphasize the Art of Active Listening:** This ensures clear skies and calm waters through understanding.
- **Establish Norms of Respect:** Laying the foundation of respectful communication charts a course away from the rocks of misunderstanding.
- **Promote Regular Care for the Ship and Crew: We can** proactively mend small rifts before they become gaping holes.
- **Foster a Safe Environment:** Creating a space where the crew feels safe sharing their fears and hopes prevents conflicts from brewing from silence and secrecy.

Ask the Captain

How do we spot an approaching storm of conflict?

Keep a lookout for darkening skies – changes in tone, sudden squalls of emotion, or a crewmate steering off course. Recognizing these signs early can help you adjust your sails accordingly.

What's the best way to calm the seas after a storm has passed?

Start by mending the sails together. A genuine apology or an open discussion about the voyage through the storm can help calm the waters, ensuring smoother sailing ahead.

How do we navigate conflicts when we're at the helm alone?

Trust your compass – your values and the lessons learned from past voyages. Use your skills in diplomacy and active listening to chart a course through the conflict, keeping the ship steady and the crew safe.

THE CAPTAIN'S GUIDING LIGHT

(Key Chapter Takeaways)

1. **Chart Your Own Course**: Use the stars of empathy and understanding to navigate through the night, guiding your ship towards resolution.
2. **Steady as She Goes**: Maintain your course with clear communication and an open heart, even when the seas turn rough.
3. **All Crew on Deck**: Remember, a ship sails best when the crew works together. Encourage open dialogue and shared solutions for navigating through conflicts.
4. **The Lighthouse of Reflection**: After the storm, reflect on the voyage. Each conflict resolved is a lighthouse built, guiding you and others toward safer passages.
5. **Harbor of Forgiveness**: Let the harbor of forgiveness be your destination. Releasing grudges and embracing understanding anchors you in calm waters, ready for whatever the next tide brings.

CHAPTER 39
PREVENTING CONFLICTS THROUGH PROACTIVE COMMUNICATION

Sailing through the teenage years, we're all captains of our ships, navigating the sometimes choppy waters of friendships and relationships. But rather than bracing for every potential storm, we can chart a course for smoother seas through proactive communication. By keeping the lines of communication open, setting clear markers like buoys (boundaries), and regularly scanning the horizon (emotional check-ins), we can avoid many storms that might otherwise catch us off guard.

BUILDING A COMPASS OF OPEN COMMUNICATION

Just as a ship needs a compass, open communication empowers us to steer our relationships through murky waters. Establishing this compass involves:

- **Creating a Safe Harbor**: Foster an environment where friends feel secure to share their thoughts and feelings, free from the storms of judgment or ridicule, fostering a sense of trust and comfort.

- **Navigating with Transparency**: Just as clear waters make for safe sailing, honesty in our communications ensures we avoid the hidden dangers that can damage relationships. Without transparency, misunderstandings can arise, leading to conflicts.
- **Charting with Curiosity**: Approach conversations with a sense of exploration. Asking questions can uncover new lands (perspectives) and prevent us from assuming we already know the terrain, fostering a sense of engagement and interest.

SETTING EXPECTATIONS AND BOUNDARIES

Clear expectations and boundaries are like the lighthouses guiding ships safely to shore. They illuminate our path, helping us navigate our relationships without running aground.

- **Drawing the Map Early**: Discuss and agree on what behaviors are on course and which veer off into treacherous waters. A practical tip for this is to talk with your friend or partner about your boundaries and what actions or behaviors are acceptable.
- **Adjusting the Sails**: As we journey together, our course may change. Be open to discussing and recalibrating boundaries as needed.
- **Respecting Other Ships**: Just as we expect others to steer clear of our marked waters, we must also honor the boundaries they've set. This applies to all friendships, romantic partnerships, or family relationships.

REGULAR CHECK-INS: KEEPING THE CREW TOGETHER

Just as a captain checks in with their crew, regular conversations with our mates ensure we're all sailing in the same direction.

- **Tending to Small Leaks**: Addressing minor issues early can prevent them from sinking the ship. Regular check-ins offer a chance to patch these up before they become unmanageable. For example, suppose you notice a friend becoming distant. In that case, addressing it early on is essential to prevent the issue from escalating and potentially damaging the friendship.
- **Strengthening the Bonds**: These moments help us stay connected with our crew's lives, strengthening our fellowship for the voyages ahead.
- **Adapting to the Changing Seas**: People and our journeys change. Regular conversations help our relationships evolve in harmony with these changes.

CULTIVATING A POSITIVE COMMUNICATION CULTURE

The crew's communication culture can set the tone for the entire voyage. Cultivating a positive environment involves:

- **Leading by Example**: Show the kindness, respect, and honesty you wish to see reflected in your crew.
- **Promoting Supportive Seas**: Encourage an atmosphere where every wave brings support, celebration, and empathy.
- **Correcting the Course**: When negative patterns emerge, address them directly to ensure smooth sailing ahead.

By nurturing a culture that values honest, respectful, and empathetic communication, teens can create social circles that are less prone to conflict and more supportive and understanding overall.

In this proactive approach to managing social interactions, the focus shifts from merely reacting to conflicts to preventing many disputes through thoughtful communication practices. By laying a foundation of open communication, setting clear boundaries, engaging in regular emotional check-ins, and fostering a culture of positive communication, teens can navigate their social worlds with confidence and grace. These strategies minimize the potential for misunderstandings and disagreements and enhance the overall quality of their relationships, creating a more harmonious and supportive social environment.

Ask the Captain

How do I create a safe harbor for open conversations?

Anchor in calm waters—choose a quiet, comfortable setting free from distractions. Show your crew (friends) through your actions and words that their thoughts and feelings will be met with understanding, not judgment.

What if my course needs adjusting but my crew doesn't agree?

Communication is key. Share why you feel a change in course is necessary and listen to their concerns. Sometimes, a new perspective can find a passage through seemingly impassable waters.

How can I encourage my crew to speak up when they're usually silent?

Sometimes, crew members may feel overlooked in the hustle of a busy deck. Encourage them by asking for their input directly, showing genuine interest in their thoughts, and giving them the floor without interruption.

THE CAPTAIN'S GUIDING LIGHT

(Key Chapter Takeaways)

1. **Chart Your Course with Care**: Let honesty, respect, and curiosity guide your ship, ensuring smooth sailing ahead.
2. **Set Boundaries Like Beacons**: Clear boundaries light the way, preventing your ship from veering into troubled waters.
3. **Regular Check-Ins Keep the Ship on Course**: Like checking the stars, regular emotional check-ins ensure you're navigating true to your course.
4. **Cultivate a Crew of Kindness**: Foster a ship where every sailor knows they're valued, their voice matters, and support is always at hand.
5. **Steer Clear of Stormy Seas with Positive Practices**: Negative communication can lead you into a tempest. Choose positive interactions to keep the seas calm and your journey pleasant.

CHAPTER 40
CREATING A CONFLICT RESOLUTION PLAN FOR SCHOOL

Amidst our educational vessels' bustling decks and crowded halls, disputes and disagreements are as inevitable as the changing tides. However, navigating these choppy waters requires more than an ad-hoc approach; it calls for a meticulously charted map—a formal conflict resolution plan. Such a plan ensures that every student feels seen and heard and fosters a climate of understanding and mutual respect across the entire school.

THE BEACON OF A STRUCTURED APPROACH

A structured conflict resolution plan is the lighthouse guiding our ships through foggy disputes. It illuminates a clear path forward, ensuring every member of the school crew—from the youngest sailors to the seasoned captains (students to administrators)—knows how to steer through conflicts with fairness and integrity.

MANNING THE HELM: INVOLVING ALL STAKEHOLDERS

Creating a robust conflict resolution plan requires the collective effort of the entire crew. Inviting students, teachers, and administrators to the captain's table ensures our plan reflects the diversity and complexity of our school's ecosystem. This collaborative approach anchors the plan in real-world insights and ensures it's embraced from the stern to the bow.

THE COMPASS POINTS: COMPONENTS OF AN EFFECTIVE PLAN

An effective conflict resolution plan is guided by several key compass points:

- **Clear Navigation Charts (Procedures)**: Detailed maps outlining the steps from conflict identification to resolution ensure no sailor feels adrift.
- **Trusted Navigators (Designated Mediators)**: Skilled mediators, whether faculty or peers, act as guiding stars, helping disputing parties navigate calm waters.
- **Regular Log Entries (Follow-Up Measures)**: Post-resolution check-ins ensure the conflict remains in the wake, not looming ahead.
- **Sailing Lessons (Preventive Education)**: Integrating conflict resolution skills into the school's curriculum arms every sailor with the tools needed for smooth sailing.

SETTING SAIL: IMPLEMENTATION AND EVALUATION

Bringing the conflict resolution plan to life is akin to embarking on a maiden voyage. Starting with test sails in select parts of the school allows for course corrections based on the crew's feedback. Training for mediators and workshops for the school community ensure everyone is ready to navigate according to the new map. Continuously evaluating and updating our course based on the changing seas keeps our plan relevant and effective.

Ask the Captain

How do we choose our navigators (mediators)?

Select crew members who are not only respected on deck but also possess a keen sense of fairness and empathy. Training in the art of mediation will ensure they're ready to guide their fellow sailors through storms to peace.

What if the conflict involves a crew member and a captain (student and teacher)?

In such cases, it's crucial to have an impartial admiral (external mediator) step in, ensuring the process remains fair and unbiased, allowing both voices to be heard equally.

How do we keep our conflict resolution plan from becoming outdated?

Regularly convene the crew for feedback sessions and review the currents (current issues) facing the school. Updating the plan based on these insights ensures it remains a reliable compass.

THE CAPTAIN'S GUIDING LIGHT

(Key Chapter Takeaways)

1. **Steady as She Goes**: Patience and consistency are your best mates in implementing the plan.
2. **All Hands on Deck**: Involve every member of the school in shaping and supporting the conflict resolution plan.
3. **Navigate with Empathy**: Always steer through conflicts with an understanding heart and an open mind.
4. **Chart New Courses**: Be open to adjusting your conflict resolution strategies based on the changing tides of the school environment.
5. **The Captain's Log**: Keep detailed records of conflicts and resolutions to guide future navigations.

PART FIVE
STANDING STRONG: THE ROOTS OF SELF-ESTEEM

Picture a towering, ancient tree, its roots sprawling deep and wide beneath the earth. Like this tree, our self-esteem has its roots, reaching the depths of our experiences, beliefs, and the world around us. These roots, whether nourished or neglected, shape the strength and resilience of our self-worth, influencing how we stand in the face of life's storms. This chapter peels back the layers of soil to explore the intricate root system of self-esteem, offering insights and strategies to foster a healthy, flourishing sense of self.

CHAPTER 41
FOUNDATION OF SELF-WORTH

In the vast ocean of life, the ship of our self-esteem sails, guided by internal compasses and external winds. This journey through choppy waters and calm seas not only tests but also strengthens the resilience of our vessel—our sense of self-worth. Below deck, personal achievements and setbacks are the ballast, giving weight and balance to our journey, while above deck, the social currents and familial winds push us towards or away from the shores of confidence. This ship, our self-esteem, is not a fragile vessel but a resilient one, capable of adapting to the changing tides of life.

CHARTING THE COURSE: ACHIEVEMENTS AND FAILURES

Our voyages are marked by triumphs and trials, each leaving its mark on the hull of our self-esteem. The moments we navigate successfully bolster our confidence, like a favorable wind propelling us forward. However, when we find ourselves adrift after a setback, it's not the end of our journey but a chance to chart a new course. Viewing failures not as setbacks but as opportunities to learn and adjust our sails instills in us a sense of hope and optimism.

It allows us to navigate future waters with more excellent skill and resilience, knowing that each failure is a stepping stone towards personal growth.

THE LURE OF SOCIAL MEDIA SEAS

Sailing the social media seas is like being caught in a whirlpool of comparison, where every glance at another's vessel makes ours seem less seaworthy. Yet, recognizing these waters for the mirage they often are—a highlight reel of another's journey—can help steer us back to our own path. It's important to curate our social media maps to include beacons of authenticity and relatability, as they can guide us through these deceptive currents, just like a lighthouse guides a ship in the dark.

THE HARBOR OF FAMILY AND COMMUNITY

The port from which we set sail, family and community, anchors our sense of self. Supportive harbors foster a strong and resilient ship, while turbulent docks can leave us feeling unseaworthy. For sailors seeking calmer waters, the guidance of mentors, educators, and community groups can offer safe harbors, reinforcing our vessel's integrity and preparing us for the open seas. The sense of belonging and security that these communities provide is crucial in building and maintaining our self-esteem, making us feel valued and supported.

Ask the Captain

How do I keep my ship steady in the storm of comparison?

Chart your own course, young sailor. Remember, the strength of your vessel lies in its uniqueness. Navigate by your own stars, not by the lights of others.

What do I do when a failure breaches my hull?

Patch it up with lessons learned, and set sail again. Each breach teaches us where our ship needs strengthening, turning setbacks into steps towards a sturdier build.

How can I find a supportive crew when my harbor is stormy?

Look to the lighthouses—mentors and community groups that stand as beacons of guidance and support. Their light can guide you to a crew that shares your journey.

Ask the Captain

THE CAPTAIN'S GUIDING LIGHT

(Key Chapter Takeaways)

1. **Celebrate Every Milestone**: No victory is too small in the voyage of self-growth. Each one is a star by which to navigate.
2. **Embrace the Winds of Challenge**: Let the gales of difficulty fill your sails, pushing you towards new skills and understandings.
3. **Seek Out Your Compass Points**: Surround yourself with those who reflect the true north of who you aspire to be.
4. **Chart Your Own Map**: Your journey is yours alone. Draw your map not by the courses others have taken, but by your own dreams and values.
5. **Keep Your Lighthouse in View**: Remember the core of who you are, your values, and your strengths. They are the light that guides you home.

CHAPTER 42
POSITIVE SELF-TALK FOR A CONFIDENT SELF-IMAGE

Amidst the vast seas of our thoughts, where whispers of doubt and billows of confidence clash, steering our vessel toward the shores of positive self-image requires a skilled navigator. Like a relentless storm, negative self-talk can veer us off course, obscuring the sunlit paths of self-appreciation and esteem. Yet, with a firm hand on the helm and an eye on the horizon, we can chart a course through these turbulent waters, cultivating an inner dialogue that buoys our spirits and anchors our confidence.

NAVIGATING THROUGH NEGATIVE MISTS

To steer our course toward more positive currents, we must first identify the fog of negative self-talk, actively using our compass of awareness to detect and dispel these misty veils:

- **Vigilance on the Voyage**: Watch for shadowy islands of self-doubt and negative whispers, marking them on your mental map for avoidance.

- **Questioning the Wind's Whispers**: Challenge the gusts of negativity that fill your sails; are they the actual winds of reality or just tempests of perception?
- **Recharting Your Course**: With each negative thought spotted on the horizon, plot a new course with a positive counter-current, steering your thoughts towards calmer waters.

A GROWTH MINDSET

Developing a growth mindset is like harnessing the favorable wind that propels us forward, turning challenges into opportunities for development and learning. It's a beacon of hope that guides us through the stormy seas of self-doubt and negativity.

- **Embrace the Squall**: See every challenge as an uncharted island ripe for exploration and discovery.
- **Persevere through Stormy Seas**: When setbacks threaten to capsize your resolve, remember that each wave overcome strengthens your ship.
- **Celebrate the Journey, Not Just the Destination**: Recognize that each stroke of the oar and each mile traversed contributes to your growth as a seasoned sailor.

GUIDING STARS OF VISUALIZATION AND AFFIRMATION

The stars of visualization and affirmations guide us through the night, illuminating our path toward achieving our dreams:

- **Envisioning Safe Harbors**: Picture yourself reaching your goals, the shores of your aspirations vivid on the horizon, guiding you through the darkest nights.

- **Chanting Sea Shanties of Self-Belief**: Sing the songs of affirmations, melodies of self-assurance, and capability to keep your spirits high and your course true.

THE ANCHOR OF SELF-COMPASSION

In tumultuous seas, self-compassion is the anchor that steadies our vessel, reminding us to treat ourselves with the same kindness and understanding we would show a shipmate in distress. It's a gentle reminder to be patient and forgiving with ourselves, especially in the face of self-doubt and criticism.

- **Kindness in the Gale**: Speak to yourself with the warmth of a calm breeze, even when the gales of criticism howl.
- **Unity in the Voyage**: Remember, all sailors face storms; you are not alone in navigating these waters.
- **Mindfulness in the Helm**: Hold the wheel with mindfulness, acknowledging the present waves without letting them dictate your course.

Self-compassion offers a gentle reminder that we are all works in progress who are deserving of patience and kindness, especially from ourselves. This practice not only nurtures a healthy self-image but also equips us with the emotional resilience to face life's challenges with grace.

In tending to the garden of our minds, we learn that positive self-talk, a growth mindset, visualization, and self-compassion are not just tools for cultivating self-confidence but are also acts of self-love. They remind us that we are capable of growth, deserving of kindness, and equipped to achieve our dreams. As we replace the weeds of negative self-talk with the flora of positivity, we create a mental landscape where a confident self-image can flourish, unencumbered by doubt and nourished by belief in our potential.

Ask the Captain

How do I silence the storm of negative self-talk?

Acknowledge the storm, then adjust your sails. Each thought of doubt is but a gust; steer your thoughts towards the lighthouse of your strengths.

Can a true sailor thrive without ever facing a storm?

It is through weathering storms that a sailor's skill is honed. Embrace each squall as a teacher and you'll emerge a master of the seas.

What if my compass seems broken and positive thoughts feel out of reach?

Even the most experienced navigators need to recalibrate their compasses. Seek out stars of positivity in the simpler things and let them guide you back to course.

THE CAPTAIN'S GUIDING LIGHT

(Key Chapter Takeaways)

1. **Chart Your Achievements**: Record the milestones of your journey, big or small, as reminders of how far you've sailed.
2. **Seek New Horizons**: Embrace the unknown with curiosity, letting the thrill of discovery fuel your voyage.
3. **Gather Your Crew**: Surround yourself with fellow voyagers who share your thirst for positive seas, supporting each other through thick and thin.
4. **Learn the Language of the Seas**: Educate yourself in the art of positive self-talk; let every word be a sail pushing you forward.
5. **Treasure Your Journey**: Remember, each wave overcome, each storm weathered, adds to the treasure chest of your experiences. Value these above all.

CHAPTER 43
PEER PRESSURE: RECOGNIZING AND RESISTING

While sailing the turbulent seas of adolescence, we often encounter the strong currents of peer pressure. These forces can push us away from our true north, tempting us to navigate away from the paths we've charted based on our values and beliefs. Recognizing and resisting these currents is essential for maintaining our course and ensuring our voyage through these years leads us to the shores of integrity and self-assuredness.

IDENTIFYING THE CURRENTS OF INFLUENCE

Peer pressure, like the ocean's currents, comes in various forms, each with its unique challenges:

- **Direct Waves**: These are the precise, forceful pushes from peers to act in specific ways, as visible as a storm on the horizon.
- **Undercurrents**: Subtler than direct waves, these pressures are the unspoken expectations and norms that flow beneath the surface of our social circles.

Recognizing these patterns helps sailors anticipate and navigate them, keeping their vessels steady and on course.

NAVIGATING THROUGH PRESSURE

When facing the gales of influence, a sturdy helm and a precise compass bearing are vital:

- **Steadfast Decision Making**: Anchoring in your values helps maintain your course through the choppiest waters.
- **Assertive Communication**: Hoisting your flag with clarity and confidence allows you to express your position without being swept away by the currents.
- **A Crew of Allies**: Sailing with a crew who shares your navigational chart – your values and beliefs – provides support and strength to resist the pressures of conformity.

SEEKING PORTS OF SUPPORT

In the vast ocean of adolescence, finding harbors of like-minded peers offers respite and reinforcement:

- **Familiar Waters**: Align with those who sail similar seas, sharing interests and values that resonate with your compass.
- **Mutual Respect**: Building a crew on the foundation of mutual respect ensures that every voice is heard and valued, steering clear of the shoals of judgment.
- **Open Channels**: Maintaining open lines of communication among your crew fosters an environment where all can navigate freely, without fear of the undercurrents of peer pressure.

PRACTICING MANEUVERS WITH ROLE-PLAYING

Training in calm waters prepares us for the turbulent ones. Role-playing scenarios offer a safe harbor to practice steering through peer pressure:

- **Charting Scenarios**: Map out various situations you might face, from invitations to navigate into the stormy waters of risky behavior to the subtle drifts toward unwanted destinations.
- **Strategizing Responses**: For each mapped scenario, chart a course of responses. Practice turning into the wind with assertive refusals or setting a new course with alternative suggestions.
- **Feedback Compass**: After each practice, ask your crew to provide feedback, adjusting the sails and refining your course based on their insights to ensure more vital navigation skills for future encounters.

Incorporating these elements into the battle against peer pressure equips teens with the tools to navigate these challenges. By understanding the types of peer pressure, asserting themselves with confidence, fostering supportive friendships, and practicing role-playing, teens can maintain their integrity and independence in the face of conformity pressures. These strategies not only help in resisting unwanted influences but also in building a sense of self that's anchored in personal values and respect.

Ask the Captain

How do I stay true to my course when the currents of peer pressure are strong?

Anchor deep in your values and trust your compass. Even the strongest currents can't move a ship that's anchored firmly.

What if my crew wants to sail into a storm I know is dangerous?

It's okay to choose a different course. A true crew respects each captain's decision to navigate their own vessel.

How can I find a crew that shares my navigational chart?

Send out signals of your interests and values. The right crew will respond to your call, drawn by the shared stars you navigate by.

THE CAPTAIN'S GUIDING LIGHT

(Key Chapter Takeaways)

1. **Set Your Compass**: Regularly check in with your values and beliefs. They are your compass on this voyage, guiding you through fog and clear skies alike.

2. **Map Your Journey**: Keep a log of your travels – the challenges you face and the victories you achieve. Reflecting on your journey helps you navigate future seas with wisdom.
3. **Learn the Language of the Sea**: Master the art of assertive communication. It's the wind in your sails, propelling you forward without being pushed off course.
4. **Gather Your Charts**: Surround yourself with maps – books, mentors, and allies who have navigated these waters before. Their knowledge is your guide to avoiding known perils.
5. **Celebrate Your Voyage**: Each day at sea is a victory. Celebrate the journey, not just the destination. The skills you hone and the sights you see are treasures to be valued.

CHAPTER 44
THE INFLUENCE OF SOCIAL MEDIA ON SELF-ESTEEM

In the vast ocean of digital interaction, social media platforms are like islands where individuals cast their messages in bottles into the sea, hoping to connect with distant shores. Yet, these islands can also be mirrors, reflecting back at us an image that sometimes distorts our self-perception. Understanding the ebb and flow of social media's influence on our self-esteem is crucial for maintaining a steady course through the sometimes stormy waters of adolescence.

SOCIAL MEDIA AND SELF-REFLECTION

Amidst the constant stream of posts and pictures, it's crucial to pause and reflect. It's easy to feel adrift in a sea of comparison, where the carefully curated highlights of others' lives can make our own seem dull. But remember, each post is just a snapshot, revealing only a fraction of the whole story. We must remind ourselves that behind each image lies a world as intricate and multifaceted as ours.

CHARTING A MINDFUL COURSE

To steer clear of the shoals of unfavorable comparison, mindful navigation of these digital waters is essential:

- **Curate Your Crew**: Follow accounts that uplift, inspire, and cast away those who bring you down.
- **Set Sails, Not Anchors**: Use features to limit your time on these platforms. Designate specific times to catch the wind in your sails without getting caught in the current of endless scrolling.
- **Signal, Don't Scroll**: Engage actively with the content that resonates with you. Signal to others through comments and shares, forging genuine connections on this vast sea.

EMBARKING ON A DIGITAL DETOX

Periodically docking your ship from the digital harbor and taking a voyage into the real world can refresh your spirit and perspective:

- **Rediscover the Horizon**: Use this time to explore interests and activities that reconnect you with the tangible world around you.
- **Navigate Your Digital Map**: Reflect on your online journey and its impact on your well-being, adjusting your course as necessary.
- **Savor the Voyage**: Embrace the present moment, finding joy in life's simple, unfiltered beauty.

CREATING A POSITIVE ONLINE PRESENCE

While social media can challenge our self-esteem, it also offers opportunities to craft an online presence that reflects our authentic selves and uplifts others. Here are some tips for achieving this:

- **Share Your Real Life:** Don't shy away from posting about your struggles or failures alongside your successes. This authenticity contributes to a more positive social media environment. It resonates with others, fostering a sense of community and shared humanity.
- **Celebrate Others:** Make a habit of supporting and celebrating your friends' and followers' achievements and milestones. Positive engagement creates a ripple effect, encouraging an atmosphere of kindness and support.
- **Advocate for Causes You Believe In:** Use your platform to raise awareness about issues close to your heart. Whether environmental conservation, mental health awareness, or social justice, your advocacy can inspire action and bring about meaningful change.

In navigating the complex relationship between social media and self-esteem, it becomes clear that mindful engagement with these platforms can transform them from sources of comparison and self-doubt to tools for connection, inspiration, and positive self-expression. By curating our feeds, taking regular breaks, and fostering a genuine online presence, we not only protect our self-esteem but also empower ourselves to navigate these digital waters with confidence and control.

Ask the Captain

How do I stay afloat amidst the waves of comparison?

Remember, every sailor faces their own storms. Focus on navigating your own ship, and use others' beacons as guidance, not benchmarks.

How can I find my crew in the vast ocean of social media?

Send out signals that reflect your true self and interests. Those on a similar course will find you, drawn by the authenticity of your beacon.

What if I lose my way in the digital fog?

Drop anchor and take time to consult your map. Reflection away from the digital world can help clear the fog and reveal your true course.

THE CAPTAIN'S GUIDING LIGHT

(Key Chapter Takeaways)

1. **Anchor in Authenticity**: Let your true self be your compass, guiding your interactions and posts.
2. **Celebrate All Voyages**: Use your platform to shine a light on the achievements and challenges of your digital crew, fostering a community of support.
3. **Navigate with Kindness**: Approach both your own posts and interactions with others from a place of empathy and understanding.
4. **Set Boundaries Like Coastlines**: Know when to dock your ship and take a break from the digital seas to maintain your well-being.
5. **Explore Uncharted Waters**: Use social media to discover new interests and perspectives, expanding your horizon beyond the familiar.

CHAPTER 45
ROLE MODELS AND MENTORS: FINDING YOUR PATH

In the voyage of youth, amidst the swirling currents of growth and change, the lighthouses of role models and mentors stand as beacons of guidance and inspiration. Their wisdom lights up uncharted waters, helping teens confidently steer their ships toward the shores of their potential.

THE COMPASS OF ROLE MODELS

Role models shine like stars in the night sky, guiding us by example. They embody the virtues we strive for and the ambitions we aim to achieve. Whether a historical figure's steadfast determination or a community leader's compassionate deeds, these guiding lights encourage us to sail through storms and reach our dreams. They remind us that, though the seas may be rough, perseverance and integrity can navigate us to our desired destinations.

NAVIGATING WITH MENTORS

While role models inspire from a distance, mentors offer hands-on guidance, charting a course alongside us. These seasoned navigators share their maps, pointing out potential hazards and highlighting routes to success. Finding a mentor starts with recognizing the areas you seek knowledge in—be it academic, professional, or personal waters—and extending a hand to those who have sailed those seas before. Schools and community groups often harbor such connections, ready to set sail when you are. Remember:

- **Signal Your Intentions**: Raise your flag to show you're seeking guidance. Reach out to potential mentors with a clear message in a bottle, outlining the shores you aim to explore.
- **Chart Your Course Together**: Share your navigational charts—your goals—with your mentor, allowing them to plot points along your journey that align with your aspirations.
- **Welcome the Weather Ahead**: Embrace the winds of feedback, adjusting your sails accordingly. Every gust teaches you to navigate more skillfully.

BECOMING A BEACON

As you journey, you, too, can shine as a beacon for fellow voyagers. Displaying qualities like courage, kindness, and understanding makes you a role model in the eyes of your crewmates. Whether steering a project at school or volunteering in your community, your actions can inspire others to follow the stars of their own aspirations.

LEARNING FROM THE WIDE OCEAN

The vast sea of life is richer for its diversity. Engaging with role models and mentors from varied backgrounds and with diverse experiences broadens your horizon, inviting you to see the world through a kaleidoscope of perspectives. This wealth of understanding cultivates a spirit of inclusivity and empathy, essential for navigating the complex waters of our global community.

- **Seek Variety:** Actively look for role models and mentors from diverse cultures, professions, and life paths.
- **Ask Questions:** Use your time with mentors to inquire about their experiences, challenges, and perspectives. Genuine curiosity opens doors to deeper understanding.
- **Reflect on Differences:** Consider how their experiences differ from yours and what lessons you can draw from them to apply to your life.

As we wrap up this exploration of the pivotal roles that role models and mentors play in guiding teens through the formative years of their lives, we're reminded of the power of connection, guidance, and inspiration in shaping our paths. These relationships illuminate the possibilities that lie ahead and instill the confidence and determination needed to pursue them. With the insights gleaned from those we admire and the support of those who believe in us, we're better equipped to navigate the challenges of adolescence and beyond, carving out our unique journeys with purpose and passion.

Looking ahead, the journey of self-discovery and growth continues, with each step offering new opportunities to learn, evolve, and contribute to the world around us.

Ask the Captain

How do I find my North Star in a sea of influences?

Chart by your values, young sailor. In the vast sky of possibilities, your true North Star shines in alignment with what matters most to you. Seek those who reflect this light.

What if my course changes while following a role model?

Ah, the sea is ever-changing, and so are we. It's natural for your course to evolve. Role models inspire us to set sail, but your journey is your own. Adjust your compass as you grow.

How can I be a lighthouse for others when I'm still navigating my own path?

Even the brightest lighthouses were once seeking their light. Share the lessons from your voyage so far; your experiences can guide others, just as you look to the stars for guidance.

THE CAPTAIN'S GUIDING LIGHT

(Key Chapter Takeaways)

1. **Harbor of Honesty**: In your dealings and self-reflections, let honesty be your anchor, keeping you grounded in integrity.
2. **Winds of Willpower**: Let determination fill your sails as you pursue your goals, knowing that it is those who dared to dream who have navigated the seas.
3. **Compass of Compassion**: Show kindness to fellow voyagers, understanding that everyone's sea is stormy at times.
4. **Telescope of Tenacity**: Keep your focus on the horizon, even when waves rise high. Your persistence is the telescope that brings distant dreams within sight.
5. **Chart of Change**: Embrace the shifting tides of life, adapting your course as you learn and grow. Change is the chart that leads to new discoveries.

Please Share Your Feedback

Congratulations on completing "Essential Social Skills for Teens"! We hope the knowledge and strategies shared have empowered you to navigate social situations with confidence and empathy. Your feedback is invaluable, so please consider leaving a review on Amazon to help shape the book's future and benefit other teens.

Scan the QR code below or visit the link to access the review page.

https://www.amazon.com/review/create-review/?asin=B0D3CPYSGG

Thank you for your support, and may your newfound social skills empower you to thrive in all aspects of your life.

With gratitude,

Jordan

CONCLUSION

In the voyage of self-discovery and growth, *Essential Social Skills for Teens* has charted a course through the sometimes tumultuous seas of the teenage years, offering a compass for personal development, resilience, and understanding. Across the four parts and forty-five chapters, this guide illuminates the path for navigating complex emotional landscapes, fostering healthy relationships, and building a sturdy foundation of self-worth and confidence.

From the initial exploration of emotional intelligence and the art of assertive communication to the deeper dive into managing peer pressure and the influence of social media, each chapter has been a beacon, guiding readers through both internal challenges and external pressures. The journey has emphasized the importance of empathy, not just as a tool for understanding others but as a cornerstone for self-compassion and growth.

Through practical advice on dealing with conflicts, embracing one's unique journey, and the significance of mentors and role models, this guide has prepared teens to sail confidently into their futures. Including interactive elements, such as "Ask the Captain" and

"Captain's Guiding Lights," has provided actionable steps and wisdom to apply in daily life, ensuring that the lessons learned are both theoretical and lived experiences.

At its heart, *Essential Social Skills for Teen*s serves as a reminder that the teenage years, while often marked by stormy waters, are also ripe with opportunities for discovery, learning, and profound personal growth. With the right tools, resilience, and support, teens can thrive, setting a course for a fulfilling journey into adulthood.

As the final page turns on this guide, the voyage doesn't end; it merely marks the beginning of countless new adventures on the horizon. Armed with knowledge, empathy, and a sense of purpose, teens are encouraged to chart their own paths, knowing that their challenges are stepping stones to becoming the captains of their destinies. The journey of adolescence, with all its trials and triumphs, is a testament to the resilience of the human spirit, a voyage that, while individual, is universally shared and deeply connected to the stories of those who have navigated these waters before.

REFERENCES

- Protect your digital footprint, protect your future. Retrieved from https://temple-news.com/protect-your-digital-footprint-protect-your-future/
- The Ultimate Guide On How To Manage Social Media Privacy Settings. Retrieved from https://www.socialpilot.co/blog/ultimate-guide-manage-social-media-privacy-settings
- Cyberbullying: What is it and how to stop it. Retrieved from https://www.unicef.org/end-violence/how-to-stop-cyberbullying
- How Screen Time Affects Teens: Mental Health and More. Retrieved from https://adventisthealth.org/blog/2023/august/how-screen-time-affects-teens-mental-health-and-/
- Assertive Vs Aggressive - Counseling, Therapy and More. Retrieved from https://www.lodestonecenter.com/assertive-vs-aggressive/
- Being assertive: Reduce stress, communicate better. Retrieved from https://www.mayoclinic.org/healthy-lifestyle/stress-management/in-depth/assertive/art-20044644
- The Importance of Personal Boundaries. Retrieved from https://psychcentral.com/relationships/the-importance-of-personal-boundaries
- 7 Key Components of Assertive Body Language for Leaders. Retrieved from https://www.risely.me/top-components-of-assertive-body-language/
- Teaching Emotional Intelligence to Teens and Students. Retrieved from https://positivepsychology.com/teaching-emotional-intelligence/
- Active listening with pre-teens and teenagers. Retrieved from https://raisingchildren.net.au/pre-teens/communicating-relationships/communicating/active-listening
- Conveying Empathy in Telephonic and Digital Communication. Retrieved from https://journals.lww.com/professionalcasemanagementjournal/fulltext/2020/09000/conveying_empathy_in_telephonic_and_digital.9.aspx
- 5 tips for dealing with online trolls - ReachOut Australia. Retrieved from https://au.reachout.com/articles/5-tips-for-dealing-with-trolls
- Effective Guide to Conflict Resolution for Teenagers. Retrieved from https://esoftskills.com/conflict-resolution-for-teens/
- Help your teenager develop empathy - ReachOut Parents. Retrieved from https://parents.au.reachout.com/common-concerns/everyday-issues/things-to-try-bullying-behaviour/help-your-teenager-develop-empathy

REFERENCES

- Youth Peer Mediation Workbook | Training Kids To Resolve Conflicts. Retrieved from https://www.youthpeermediation.com/
- The Power and the Pain of Adolescents' Digital Experiences. Retrieved from https://www.ncbi.nlm.nih.gov/pmc/articles/PMC5325156/
- Social Media's Effect on Self-Esteem: How Does It Affect Us? Retrieved from https://socialmediavictims.org/mental-health/self-esteem/
- Resilience for teens: 10 tips to build skills on bouncing back. Retrieved from https://www.apa.org/topics/resilience/bounce-teens
- Family Environment and Self-Esteem Development. Retrieved from https://www.ncbi.nlm.nih.gov/pmc/articles/PMC7080605/
- Peer Pressure: Strategies to Help Teens Handle it Effectively. Retrieved from https://parentandteen.com/handle-peer-pressure/

Made in United States
Orlando, FL
05 July 2025